Eight Studies Introducing
the Bible as a Whole

The Unfolding Drama of the Bible

BERNHARD W. ANDERSON

Third Edition

Fortress Press   Philadelphia

Library of Congress Cataloging-in-Publication Data

Anderson, Bernhard W.
  The unfolding drama of the Bible.

  Previously published: New York: Association Press, 1971.
  Bibliography: p.
  1. Bible—Text-books. I. Title.
  BS605.2.A5   1988   220.6   87-45884
  ISBN 0-8006-2098-4

Printed in the United States of America   1-2098

96   95   94   93   92   6   7   8   9   10

To the L.Q.L.

Contents

Preface to the
Third Edition

This study guide, which aims to help the reader understand the full sweep of the Bible from beginning to end, was originally prepared for the 1952 Religion in Life program at Bucknell University, sponsored by the Christian Association. To the surprise of many, including the author, it proved to have a wide appeal, far beyond the circle for whom it was originally intended. With the encouragement of leaders of the Student Christian Movement, this Bucknell Study Guide was issued in revised form as a Haddam House Book in 1953 and later was reprinted with only slight changes as a Reflection Book in 1957. Then in 1971 a second edition appeared that incorporated revisions based on almost two decades of use.

When the second edition ran out of print, Dr. John A. Hollar of Fortress Press responded to the requests of numerous individuals and took the lead toward reissuing the book in a form suitable for further use in the years ahead. Indeed, he has gone through the book carefully and has made many valuable editorial suggestions. As in the case of the second edition, my policy has been to retain the basic outline and as much of the original text as possible. The most noticeable changes are that the discussion conforms to current standards of inclusive language with respect to men and women and that bibliographical references have been updated to take into account ongoing scholarly research. Also, I have added a Postscript, "The Dramatic Movement of Scripture," that appeared previously in the *Union Seminary Quarterly Review* 42 (1988). It will enable readers to get some idea of how I came to be an advocate of the approach to the Bible used in this study guide.

The survival of this book through the decades is a clear indication that the study of the Bible is not a passing fad but remains a vital source of understanding for the community of faith and an irresistible challenge to many who seek for a faith that is adequate to our times. Through my career, ever since my days at the College of the Pacific, in California, I have been identified with a group known as the L.Q.L., or Life Questers' League. Members of this group have kept in touch with one another through the hastening years, and since 1980 have come together in annual retreats for study, fellowship, and worship. To this extraordinary group I dedicate this work with the hope that others will find the study of the Bible helpful in the quest for a more abundant life.

Bernhard W. Anderson
Yale Divinity School
Spring 1988

Introducing the
Bible Study

In one of his well-known sonnets John Keats tells how in reading Chapman's translation of Homer he experienced the elation of a new discovery:

> Then felt I like some watcher of the skies
> When a new planet swims into his ken;
> Or, like stout Cortez, when with eagle eyes
> He stared at the Pacific—and all his men
> Looked at each other with a wild surmise—
> Silent, upon a peak in Darien.

In our time many have had a similar experience in encountering the Bible. Bible study, of the kind you are about to engage in, can have the result of opening your eyes to a startling new vista, of giving you a new perspective upon the meaning of your life and your place in the whole historical drama.

There are two ways to study the Bible. The first is appropriate to classroom or academic study. Using this approach, one *looks at* the Bible from the outside as a spectator. One learns many interesting things about the Bible, such as the literary process which brought it to its final shape as a canon of sacred Scripture, or the cultural, archaeological, and historical background of the various books. One is curious about the ideas of the Bible, even the "idea of God," and perhaps masters these ideas well enough to pass the course with flying colors. This descriptive approach has its place, but it is not the one we shall follow in these studies.

The second approach is one in which together we shall attempt to *stand within* the Bible and to look out at the world through the window of biblical faith. Like actors who put themselves into the script of a play, we shall read the Bible with personal involvement, realizing that it is not a textbook but a "letter from God with your personal address on it," as Sören Kierkegaard once put it. We shall read it as a story which is not just about other people of long ago but which is about us in the places where we are living. The language of the Bible, when it is truly heard, can be an event, a happening, such as it was with biblical witnesses, like Moses, who first were addressed personally by the God of Abraham, Isaac, and Jacob (Exod. 3:4–6).

GOD'S MANIFESTO

The distinctiveness of this Bible study, which emphasizes the reader's identification with the plot of the story, arises from the uniqueness of the Bible itself. It is the Christian claim that the perspective set forth in the Bible has been provided by God's own self-revelation. This is what puts the Bible in a class by itself. The Bible is written not in a secret code but in living human language which reveals the dramatic involvement of God in our personal lives and in our history. Christians affirm that the Bible contains the Word of God. Just as in our everyday experience a "word" is an event of communication between persons, so God's Word is an event of communication, an act of participation in the reality of our history, as we read in John 1:14 ("The Word became flesh and dwelt among us"). This dynamic power of God's Word is a far cry from the notion that the Bible contains the literal, static words of God taken down by human stenographers. The Bible is not divine dictation but divine drama whose language poetically exposes the meaning of human life in relation to the God who has condescended to dwell among us, in our human language and history. The Bible is, to use a familiar Christian formulation, the "Word of God in human words." This conviction underlies the practice in many churches of prefacing or concluding the reading of a Scripture selection with, "The Word of the Lord."

The Bible may be described as God's Manifesto. The dictionary defines a manifesto as "a public declaration, usually of a sovereign or political group, showing intentions and motives." So, for instance, the

Communist Manifesto is a declaration of the alleged meaning of the economic struggle and the predetermined movement of the historical process toward fulfillment in a classless society. To be a communist is to understand one's existence in this context. In a more special sense the Bible is, for the Christian community, God's Manifesto. God is the Sovereign who declares the inner meaning of a historical crisis and discloses the direction of the whole human drama. God's revelation is given in the events of which the Bible is the record and the witness, events which come to climax and fulfillment in Jesus Christ. And to be a Christian is to understand one's existence in this dramatic context.

Now, this does not mean that one has to be a convinced Christian before anything can be gotten out of the study of the Bible. As Paul Lehmann once observed, "The Bible has a curious slant in favor of the unbeliever; the unbeliever, that is, who is really honest about his unbelief, and really curious about the full diversity and complexity of the world in which he lives."[1]

The only condition for fruitful Bible study is that you come with an infinite concern about the question "What is the meaning of my life, and the historical crisis in which I and my community are involved?"

- You must be willing to let the past—this biblical past—speak to you where you are living, to make a claim upon you in the present.
- You must meet others in the group as persons, respecting their individuality and being willing to learn from the conversation.
- You must come with the intention of wrestling seriously and honestly with the meaning of a biblical passage—not to air your private opinions or prejudices.
- You must be ready to hear what the great teachers of the church have had to say in their commentaries—Augustine, Calvin, Luther, and others, including those of our own period.
- You must expect to be questioned by the Bible, even as you bring your own questions to the Bible.

It may be that in this give-and-take experience you will discover an entirely new dimension of life, as you find yourself drawn into the history which God is making.

---

1. Paul Lehmann, *The Death of Jesus Christ: A Bible Study on What Led Christians to Study the Bible* (United Student Christian Council, 1951).

THE BIBLE AS A WHOLE

In this study guide we shall tackle the whole Bible. This may seem as foolish as American tourists who breeze through the Louvre as though they are trying to establish a new track record. It is admitted at the outset that this approach runs the risk of superficiality. It is hoped that you will have time enough to stake your claims so that later you can come back to sink your shafts more deeply, aided perhaps by the "Suggestions for Further Reading" given at the end of each study unit. Many people, however, lack any awareness of the Bible as a whole. They know a few snatches of Scripture here and there, like the twenty-third Psalm or the Sermon on the Mount, but are very hazy—if not completely ignorant—about the larger dramatic context within which these favorite passages have meaning. We all need to stand back from the trees so that we may see the woods. That is the justification for this study of the Bible in eight units.

In the following pages we shall consider the Bible as presenting a historical drama.[2] To be sure, this figure of speech is not found anywhere in the Bible itself, but it is a convenient and appropriate way to view the Bible as a whole. Several characteristics of a drama immediately spring to mind. For one thing, a drama has a beginning and an end; it starts somewhere and goes somewhere. Also, it has a cast of persons and the story deals with the whole range of human experience, from triumph to tragedy. Furthermore, a drama has a plot which moves forward through several acts toward a denouement (or climax) in which the episodes that took place at the beginning are understood in their larger meaning. In a drama there is a great deal of diversity: different personalities, different attitudes toward life, different episodes which take place at different times and in various settings. But underlying all this variety is the movement of the plot toward its resolution.

The Bible, too, has a unity like that of a great drama. It moves from beginning to end, from creation to new creation. The story deals with people's hopes and fears, their joy and anguish, their ambitions and

---

2. Some interpreters use the term "redemptive history" or "salvation history" (German: *Heilsgeschichte*). See Will Herberg's illuminating essay "Biblical Faith as *Heilsgeschichte*," listed at the end of this Introduction. See also the Postscript to this book, "The Dramatic Movement of Scripture," pp. 89–93 below.

failures. There is a great deal of diversity in the Bible: different authors, different historical situations, different kinds of theological expression. But underlying all this great variety is the dynamic movement, similar to the plot of a drama, which binds the whole together. The biblical drama, however, is unique in that God appears in the cast. Not only is God the Author who stands behind the scenes prompting and directing the drama but God also enters onto the stage of history as the Chief Actor—the protagonist. The biblical plot is the working out of God's purpose for the creation in spite of all efforts to oppose it. The denouement is reached, according to the conviction of the Christian community, when the crucifixion and resurrection of Jesus of Nazareth are proclaimed as the sign of God's decisive victory. In the light of this climactic event the earlier stages of the story are understood with a deeper and larger meaning.

A DRAMA IN THREE ACTS

Our series of eight studies will follow this dramatic scheme:

Prologue	In the Beginning	Study I
Act I	The Formation of God's People	
Scene 1	A Way into the Future	Study II
Scene 2	The Discipline of Disaster	Study III
Act II	The Re-formation of God's People	
Scene 1	The New Exodus	Study IV
Scene 2	The People of the Torah	Study V
Act III	The Transformation of God's People	
Scene 1	Victory through Defeat	Study VI
Scene 2	The Church in the World	Study VII
Epilogue	In the End	Study VIII

It ought to become clear that each of the acts in the dramatic scheme interprets a decisive historical event which is proclaimed as a "mighty act" of God. The three crucial moments in the biblical drama are

(1) the exodus of oppressed Israelites from Egypt and the opening of a way into the future out of a no-exit situation;

(2) the exile of conquered Israelites into Babylonia and their miraculous liberation for a new beginning in their homeland; and

(3) the crucifixion and resurrection of Jesus, which reconstituted the people of God as God's task force in the world.

The selection of passages for the study of these three major "acts" of God has to be somewhat arbitrary, for obviously we can deal with only a small fraction of the relevant biblical material. (Four passages are selected for each study unit. If only one session is devoted to each unit, the leader will have to determine which passage should be the focus of discussion. Otherwise, the group may want to stay with a particular unit for more than one session.) Our purpose is not to make an exhaustive study of the Bible but to enter into the meaning of these three crucial stages of the biblical drama.

GETTING INTO THE ACT

One final word: Do not suppose that this is the kind of drama one can view from a grandstand seat. We are not to be spectators of something that happened once upon a time. The Bible is not a book of ancient history. It is more like the commedia dell'arte, a dramatic form which flourished in sixteenth-century Italy.[3] In this kind of drama, the players were asked to improvise, to put themselves into the story. To be sure, it was not a free improvisation, for there were some given elements: there was the director, there was a company of actors, and there was a story plot which was given to them in broad outline. With these given elements they were told to improvise—that is, to fill in the gaps on their own.

In this Bible study we are called upon to improvise—that is, to put ourselves into the story and to fill in the gaps with our own experience. We must be ready to get onto the biblical stage and participate personally—along with the "company," the community of faith—in the dramatic movement of the plot, act by act. Perhaps this warning is unnecessary, for it is the testimony of many generations that when the

---

3. See my essay "The Contemporaneity of the Bible," where this point is developed, with reference to the commedia dell'arte.

Bible is read in the community of faith the Holy Spirit enhances the human words of Scripture with new meaning and power, with the result that people become actors in what Amos Wilder calls "the great story and plot of all time and space" and are drawn into relation with God, the Great Dramatist.[4]

Thus, realizing that the Great Dramatist is apt to lure us from the spectator's balcony and put us into the act, we begin our study.

Suggestions for Further Reading

Anderson, Bernhard W. The Contemporaneity of the Bible." *Princeton Seminary Bulletin* 62 (1969): 38–50.

———. "The Dramatic Movement of Scripture." *Union Seminary Quarterly Review* 42 (1988). Reprinted as the Postscript to this volume.

———. *The Living Word of the Bible.* Philadelphia: Westminster Press, 1979.

———. *Understanding the Old Testament,* 4th edition. Englewood Cliffs, N.J.: Prentice-Hall, 1986. See especially the introduction, "The Old Testament as the Story of a People." The 4th edition is cited throughout this study guide.

Brown, Robert McAffee. *The Bible Speaks to You.* Philadelphia: Westminster Press, 1955.

Brueggemann, Walter. *The Bible Makes Sense.* Atlanta: John Knox Press, 1977.

———. *The Creative Word: Canon as Model for Biblical Education.* Philadelphia: Fortress Press, 1962.

Fackre, Gabriel, *The Christian Story,* vol. 1, *A Narrative Interpretation of Basic Christian Doctrine;* vol. 2, *Authority: Scripture in the Church for the World Today* (Grand Rapids: Wm. B. Eerdmans, 1978–87). A Christian theologian maintains that doctrine gives expression to the story that unfolds in the Bible and gives it authority.

Herberg, Will. "Biblical Faith as *Heilsgeschichte:* The Meaning of Redemptive History in Human Existence." In *Faith Enacted as History: Essays in Biblical Theology,* ed. B. W. Anderson, 32–42. Philadelphia: Westminster Press, 1976.

Merton, Thomas. *Opening the Bible.* Philadelphia: Fortress Press, 1970.

Niebuhr, H. Richard. *The Meaning of Revelation.* New York: Macmillan Co., 1941. See chap. 2, "The Story of Our Life."

---

4. Amos Wilder, *The Language of the Gospel* (New York: Harper & Row, 1964), 64–65.

Sanders, James A. *Canon and Community: A Guide to Canonical Criticism.* Philadelphia: Fortress Press, 1984.

————. *Torah and Canon.* Philadelphia: Fortress Press, 1972.

Other Study Aids

Harper's Bible Dictionary. Paul J. Achtemeier, gen. ed. San Francisco: Harper & Row, 1985.

The Interpreter's One Volume Commentary on the Bible. Charles M. Laymon, ed. Nashville: Abingdon Press, 1971.

Jerome Biblical Commentary. Raymond E. Brown, J. A. Fitzmyer, and Roland Murphy, eds. Englewood Cliffs, N.J.: Prentice-Hall, 1969, new edition forthcoming.

The New English Bible with the Apocrypha: Oxford Study Edition. Samuel Sandmel, ed. New York: Oxford University Press, 1976.

The New Oxford Annotated Bible with Apocrypha. Herbert G. May and Bruce M. Metzger, eds. New York: Oxford University Press, 1973.

STUDY I

Prologue: In the Beginning

One of the daringly original themes of the biblical drama is expressed in the majestic announcement found in the first words of Genesis: "In the beginning God created the heavens and the earth." We are so used to speaking of God as Creator that we scarcely realize the revolutionary implications of this belief. According to the religions of ancient Egypt and Babylonia the gods were in nature, for nature with its creative powers (symbolized, for instance, by the sun and moon) was regarded as a manifestation of the Divine. In Babylonia, creation was seen to be caught up in a natural process which moves in a great circle toward the new creation at the turn of the year, the time of the New Year's festival. Likewise for the ancient Greeks the gods were immanent or "inside" nature, and since the cosmos was regarded as eternal there was no place in their thought for creation. The Bible stands in flat contradiction to these views. God is not immanent in nature; God is not a natural process. Rather, God is "over against" nature or, to use a philosophical term, is transcendent. Nature is not divine but displays the handiwork of its creator (Ps. 19:1), on the analogy of a painting that displays the artistry of the painter. Heaven and earth (that is, everything that is) are seen to be part of the majestic purpose of God, which moves in a vast sweep from beginning to end, from creation to consummation.[1]

LIFE'S DIMENSION OF DEPTH

A roadblock for our approach to Genesis 1–3 is our bondage to the scientific attitude. Too many people try to modernize these chapters into a scientific account, and to harmonize the narrative with modern scientific theories. Some have argued, for instance, that the "days" mentioned in Genesis 1 correspond to geological periods, or that the doctrine of evolution is implicit in the whole account (note that the emergence of biological life is associated with the waters in 1:20–23). But this is to confuse biblical language, which is poetic and imaginative, with scientific language, which is descriptive and analytical.[2] The central issue here is that of the *ultimate meaning* of human life in the natural sphere, and this is not a scientific question, properly speaking. The Bible asks—and answers—the question about human existence (the so-called existential question): "What is the origin, meaning, and destiny of human life?" One must be on guard against reading into the biblical narrative the presuppositions of our scientific age. It would be advisable to read the creation account in Genesis 1 in the context of some psalms, especially Psalms 8 and 104. This is poetic language

---

1. For further elucidation of Israel's creation belief in relation to that of ancient religions, see my *Creation versus Chaos* (Philadelphia: Fortress Press, 1987 [1967]), especially chap. 1, "Creation and History." See also my "Introduction: Mythopoeic and Theological Dimensions of Biblical Creation Faith," in *Creation in the Old Testament*, ed. B. W. Anderson (Philadelphia: Fortress Press, 1984), 1–24.

2. In some of my essays I have explored more fully the metaphorical character of biblical language: "Cosmological Dimensions of the Biblical Creation Story," supplement to *Creation versus Chaos;* "A Stylistic Study of the Priestly Creation Account," in *Canon and Authority,* ed. G. W. Coats and B. O. Long (Philadelphia: Fortress Press, 1977), 148–62; and "The Bible as Sacred Scripture," introduction to *The Books of the Bible* (New York: Charles Scribner's Sons, forthcoming).

which intends to praise the God whose purpose enfolds all things and upon whom every creature, human and nonhuman, is radically dependent for existence (see Ps. 104:27–30).[3]

It is now generally known that we have two creation stories in Genesis, the first running from Gen. 1:1 to Gen. 2:3, and the second beginning (after a transitional editorial statement, "These are the generations of . . .") with the last half of Gen. 2:4. The first of these accounts received its final literary formulation in the period of the Exile, the period we are symbolizing as Act II (about 550 B.C.), although it was probably used liturgically in temple services long before its final composition. The second account, on the other hand, comes from the period of Act I, perhaps as early as the era of Solomon (about 950 B.C.), though it probably circulated in oral tradition long before this. Each story expresses the viewpoint of the theological circle in which it was composed, just as it reflects the language and culture of its period.[4] The important thing to notice, however, is that despite the differences in style and content, both accounts affirm that the ultimate meaning of human life is disclosed not in the processes of nature but in relationship to the God who transcends the whole realm of nature. God is the Author, Sustainer, and Finisher of all that is. These stories are really word pictures that portray life's deepest dimension.

It would be helpful if we had in the English language words corresponding to the German *Weltbild,* "world picture," and *Weltanschauung,* "world perspective". The world picture of Genesis 1 is the naive one of antiquity—a picture of the earth as a flat surface, resting on the primeval "waters beneath the earth" and separated from the "waters above the earth" by a blue firmament (Gen. 2:6–7). Were it not for the Creator's sustaining power, the waters would return to their original place and engulf the world in chaos, as almost happened once upon a time, according to the flood story (Gen. 6:5—9:17; see especially 7:11–24).

The world perspective, however, concerns the meaning of the human drama enacted on the stage of nature and in relation to the natural environment. Notice that humans and animals are created on the same

---

3. See my "Creation and Worship," in *Creation versus Chaos.*

4. For a fuller discussion of these two accounts in the history of Israelite tradition, see my *Understanding the Old Testament,* 159–63, 454–60.

The Ancient Pictorial View of the Universe

 1. The waters above and below the earth
2–4. Chambers of hail, rain, snow
 5. The firmament with its "sluices"
 6. The surface of the earth
 7. The navel of the earth: "fountain of the great deep"
 8. The mountain pillars supporting the firmament
 9. Sweet waters (rivers, lakes, seas) on which the earth floats
10. Sheol, the realm of death (the "pit")

day (Gen. 1:24–28)—a fine poetic indication of humanity's involvement in, and dependence upon, the world of nature. But human beings are not just animals who live in, and adjust to, their natural environment. They are able to survey and control nature, to search for the good, the true, and the beautiful, to remember the past, to hope for the future, and to decide in the present. Elevated to a royal position "a little lower than God," as a Hebrew poet exclaimed (Ps. 8:5–8), they are given dominion over God's earthly estate (Ps. 8:5–8). The same view is expressed in Gen. 1:26–28, where at the climax of God's creation 'adam (an inclusive Hebrew word meaning "human being," "humankind") is made "in the image of God." 'Adam consists of equal partners, "male and female," who are to "image" or represent God on earth by ruling wisely and benevolently over the nonhuman creation.[5]

The story in Genesis 2 is written from a similar point of view. Like the animals, the human being ('adam) is made from the dust and returns to the dust (2:7; 3:19), but this creature's ability to name the animals indicates human superiority and dominion (2:19–20). Today we know about the chemical constituents of this dust, and we have a completely different cosmology or world picture corresponding to the dimensions of our Space Age. But have we gone beyond the biblical perspective on the meaning of human life in relation to its natural environment?

Perhaps this question becomes more forceful when we turn from biology to other fields of human endeavor, such as art, philosophy, and history. A famous historian, once a professor of modern history at the University of Cambridge, wrote some words that are relevant to the creation story. He observed that the historian does not treat humanity "as essentially a part of nature or consider [it] primarily in this aspect," as the biologist usually does. Rather, the historian "picks up the other end of the stick and envisages a world of human relations standing, so to speak, over against nature," and this leads to a study of the "new kind of life" that human beings have "superimposed on the jungle, the forest and the waste." He goes on to say, "Since this world of human relations is the historian's universe, we may say that history is a human drama

---

5. For discussion of environmental or "ecological" issues connected with the "image of God," see my "Human Dominion over Nature," in *Biblical Studies in Contemporary Thought*, ed. Miriam Ward (Somerville, Mass.: Greeno, Hadden Co., 1975), 27–45; and "Creation and Ecology," in *Creation in the Old Testament*. For an excellent commentary, turn to Walter Brueggemann, *Genesis*.

of personalities, taking place as it were on the stage of nature, and amid its imposing scenery."[6]

Thus we speak of the human drama, although often in purely humanistic terms. The creation story underscores the conviction that the drama is not just about human beings; rather, it is a "cosmic journey" which has its beginning and end in the purpose of God. Hence the whole drama is enacted within the horizons of "In the beginning God . . ." and "In the end God . . ."

PARADISE LOST

Much attention can be devoted to the narrative of paradise lost in Genesis 2 and 3, for here are to be found the profoundest insights into the human situation. Do not be disturbed by the picturesque and naive narrative style, as though this marked the story as inferior to the elevated prose of Genesis 1. Notice that the story has all the features of a good story: it has a beginning and an end; it has a cast of characters who act in relation one to another; it has a plot that dynamically moves toward a denouement or resolution. And most interesting, God, the Creator, appears as the main Actor in the story and enters into personal relationship with the man and the woman, even asking searching questions: "Where are you?" "Who told you that you were naked?" "What is this that you have done?" Reflect on the meaning of some of the symbols in the story: "one flesh," "the subtle serpent," "the tree of life," "the tree of knowledge of good and evil," nakedness, banishment from the garden, and so forth.

This is not just a story of something that happened once upon a time but is a profound description of the human situation in any historical time. The human actors—the first man and woman—represent everybody. Surely there is in human experience a melancholy awareness that life is not what it ought to be, that somehow or somewhere human beings have lost the "peace" (wholeness, well-being) and the humanness that the Creator intended. Conflict, anxiety, insecurity, exploita-

---

6. Herbert Butterfield, *Christianity and History* (New York: Charles Scribner's Sons, 1950), 6-7. For further discussion of the relation between creation and science, see the essays—including my own ("The Earth Is the Lord's")—in *Is God a Creationist? The Religious Case against Creation-Science*, ed. Roland M. Frye (New York: Charles Scribner's Sons, 1983).

tion, injustice, suffering, guilt—these are not intended to be normal, even though they are life's daily realities. Why is this? Unlike Marxism, which traces the problem to economic factors, and unlike Oriental religions (Hinduism, Buddhism) which advocate liberation from the illusory realm of sensory desire, the Bible traces the problem to something in human nature: to the human will, to human freedom. The temptation to be independent or even to be "like God" (3:5), that is, to live life in our own way and on our own terms, leads to estrangement at all levels: from God, from others, and from the earth itself.

Notice that the paradise story falls into three episodes.

In the *first* episode, the narrator portrays peace in God's beautiful garden ("paradise" is an old Persian word meaning an "enclosed park"). The human being has a God-given task: to dress and keep God's garden. Work, when performed with responsibility and dignity, is intended to be creative and fulfilling. Above all, the human being is enjoined to take care of God's garden, not to violate and pollute nature. The God-given task, however, cannot be performed alone; in fact, to quote a German proverb, Ein Mensch ist kein Mensch ("One human being is not a human at all"). So the narrator portrays the moving scene of God's creation of a woman so that the two companions may stand vis-à-vis, face to face, and even be joined in the most intimate relationship as "one flesh." The story of God's creation is not complete until *adam* is differentiated into "the man" and "the woman," the two beings who correspond to each other and who are equally responsible in caring for God's estate.[7]

In the *second* episode, the narrator portrays rebellion in the garden. The freedom that God has given the human companions places them in a situation of decision. Why be content with creaturely limitations? Why not reach out for forbidden fruit? The "theological" argument of the serpent is subtle and seductive, and the couple cannot resist the tempting possibilities of life on their own terms. The meaning of the phrase "knowing good and evil" is not altogether clear, but it seems to be a Hebrew expression for the mature and even divine wisdom required for making difficult decisions (see 1 Kings 3:9; 2 Sam. 14:17). Sin, then, is the presumption that human beings can grasp such wide and penetrating knowledge that they can live on their own resources,

---

7. See the exquisite treatment of this story from a feminist point of view by Phyllis Trible in "A Love Story Gone Awry."

without dependence upon God. Sin is a declaration of independence from God; it is the refusal to "let God be God." Above all, it should be understood that sin is not just a matter of doing something immoral, of being "bad girls and boys." Sin is, in a profound sense, a false maturity, illustrated in Jesus' parable of the prodigal son who independently goes off into a far country and wastes his substance in a life of abandon (Luke 15:11–24). The consequence, according to the paradise story, is alienation from God, from other human beings, and from one's truest self—an alienation that is rooted in a rebellious will that oversteps creaturely boundaries.

In the *third* episode (3:8–24), the narrator portrays judgment in the garden. "The love story," to use Phyllis Trible's apt words, has "gone awry." The nakedness of the man and woman exposed, they are now described as fugitives running to hide behind the trees of the garden from the Lord God, who strolls in the garden in the cool of the day. Notice the severe consequences of misused creaturely freedom. Judgment falls first upon the serpent, who proved to be more than an animal of the field—to be a symbol of the sinister power of evil. The next consequence was that the relation between the sexes was impaired: henceforth childbirth would be painful for the woman and she would be in a subordinate relation to her husband. The final consequence was that the man's work would become tedious and he would have to fight to eke out a livelihood from the soil.

The story of paradise lost ends with the picture of the two human beings, representatives of the human race, cast out from the primeval peace of the garden into a restless historical life of insecurity and conflict. The rest of the Bible, beginning with the tragic sequence of stories portrayed in Genesis 4—11 (Cain's murder of Abel, Lamech's blood revenge, violence leading to the Flood, the Tower of Babel), bears witness to the religious truth that when human beings misuse their God-given freedom they are estranged from God, from others, and from their deepest selves. For humans belong to God by nature and cannot find peace outside the relationship for which they were created. So Augustine began his *Confessions* with this prayer: "O Lord, thou has made us for thyself, and our hearts are restless until they rest in thee."

Questions to Think About

1. Discuss the difference between the "truth" of the biblical account of creation and the "truth" which we usually regard as scientific. Was it

appropriate for astronauts to broadcast as their Christmas message from the moon (Christmas 1968) the opening verses of Genesis?

2. In a famous essay, "The Historical Roots of Our Ecologic Crisis" (*Science* 155 [1967]: 1203-7; reprinted in various contexts), Lynn White, Jr., maintained that the Jewish-Christian faith is largely responsible for the present "rape of nature," because in Gen. 1:26-28 human beings are commissioned to have dominion over nature. Discuss this thesis in the light of the announcement in Genesis 1 that human beings are made in the "image" of God, or of the portrayal in Genesis 2 of the human being as the caretaker of the garden.

3. With the story of Genesis 2—3 before you, paraphrase the meaning of "sin." Can sin find expression in moral goodness as well as in immoral acts? What light, if any, does Albert Camus's novel *The Fall* throw on the story?

4. Discuss the equality of man and woman in the light of the "image of God" passage in Genesis 1 and the portrayal of man and woman as companions in the story in Genesis 2. Do you understand the story to mean that the subordination of woman was not given in God's creation but was a consequence of "the fall?"

5. A British observer, James Bryce, once observed that the American Constitution, with its system of checks and balances upon the exercise of power, was written by men who believed in "original sin." Is this realistic? Compare the Marxist view that the troubles of history are traceable to economic factors, and that when these are changed human nature will be transformed. (George Orwell's *Animal Farm* may give some food for thought.)

6. Compare the picture of creation presented in Genesis 1 with that of Psalm 104. Why is the story in Genesis 2—3 (paradise lost) a necessary supplement to the view of the human role in God's creation as set forth in Genesis 1?

Suggestions for Further Reading

Anderson, Bernhard W. "Creation and the Noachic Covenant" and "Creation and Ecology." In *The Cry of the Environment and the Rebuilding of Christian Creation Tradition*, ed. P. Joranson and K. Butigan. Santa Fe, N. Mex.: Bear & Co., 1984. The latter essay also appears in *Creation in the Old Testament*, ed. B. W. Anderson (Philadelphia: Fortress Press, 1984), 152-69.

———. *Understanding the Old Testament*, 159-66, 454-566.

Brueggemann, Walter. *Genesis,* 23-54. Atlanta: John Knox Press, 1982. Highly recommended.

Rad, Gerhard von. *Genesis.* Old Testament Library. Philadelphia: Westminster Press, 1961; revised edition, 1972. One of the best commentaries on Genesis that have appeared in the twentieth century.

Sarna, Nahum. *Understanding Genesis.* New York: McGraw-Hill, 1966;

New York: Schocken Books, 1970. A clear and illuminating exposition by a Jewish scholar.

Trible, Phyllis. "The Topical Clue" and "A Love Story Gone Awry." In *God and the Rhetoric of Sexuality.* Philadelphia: Fortress Press, 1978. An exquisite, penetrating interpretation.

Vawter, Bruce. *On Genesis: A New Reading.* New York: Doubleday & Co., 1977. A helpful commentary by a leading Roman Catholic scholar of the past generation.

A Way into the Future

Study Passages

1. Exodus 3:1–21
   The Call of Moses
2. Exodus 19:3–6; 20:1–17
   Keeping the Covenant
3. Exodus 24:3–8
   Ceremony of Covenant Making
4. Deuteronomy 4:25–40; 5:1–53; 8:1–20
   Sermonic Interpretations of Exodus and Covenant

With the exodus (the "going out") of the Israelites from Egypt, the curtain rises on the first major act of the biblical drama. Every historical community recalls some decisive event as its birth hour. Of this formative event the members of the community can say, "This is what brought us forth upon the stage of history as a people, with a shared tradition and a sense of destiny. This is where the meaning of our history was disclosed." In the United States, for instance, Americans celebrate the Revolutionary War and the signing of the Declaration of Independence as decisive events in their formation. It is significant that in a grave crisis Abraham Lincoln harked back to that creative moment: "Fourscore and seven years ago our fathers brought forth on this continent a new nation, conceived in liberty."

ISRAEL'S BIRTH HOUR

It was similar in the case of the community known as Israel, to which the church is intimately related. Still, the analogy of America and Israel breaks down for a couple of reasons. For one thing, the term "Israel," as used in the Old Testament, cannot be equated with a nation. This will come as a surprise to many because today Israel is the name of a powerful state in the Middle East, one of the members of the United Nations. But in the two centuries preceding David (about 1200–1000 B.C.), before Israel became a monarchic state "like the nations" (cf. 1 Sam. 8:4–9), the term applied to a people loosely bound in a covenant federation. And the term continued to be used of the covenant people after the fall of the nation in 587 B.C. Thus Israel, in the first and last analysis, transcends political, ethnic categories. In this larger sense Paul speaks of the community of faith, embracing both Jews and Gentiles, as the Israel of God (Gal. 5:16).

Moreover, for Israel the exodus was not just an ordinary event of history. Its meaning was perceived in a theological dimension as the event which gave them a special "calling," or vocation. The prophet Hosea used parental imagery to describe God's special relationship to this people:

> When Israel was a child, I loved him,
> and out of Egypt I called my son.
> (Hosea 11:1)

And another prophet described the exodus as the time when God created Israel to be a people so that they might perform a task in the divine purpose (Isa. 51:9–11).

It is significant that Israel's ancient confession of faith found expression in the retelling of a story in which the exodus was the focal event. The confession ran something like this: "Our ancestors were pilgrims in Palestine, wandering from place to place. A small band went down to Egypt in a time of famine, and when Israel multiplied, the Egyptian king subjected *us* to slave labor on public works. But the Lord, the God of our ancestors, saw *our* affliction and heard *our* cry. With many marvelous signs of divine concern and care, God delivered *us* from Pharaoh's yoke and brought us into a new land where we could find our freedom in the service of God." In this paraphrase of Deut. 26:5–9, note how the individual worshiper identifies with the story, as evidenced in the first personal pronouns "our," "us". Even today the Passover ceremony emphasizes the involvement of the believing Jew in that momentous event.

These crucial events, especially the central event of the Exodus, exerted a powerful influence upon the religious imagination of the people in the new situations in which they found themselves in their historical pilgrimage. The God whom Israel worships is the God who comes to a band of slaves in the time of oppression and opens a way into the future where there is no way. The imagery of the Israelite story has had a great appeal to Christians in many ages, as witnessed by the preaching of the Rev. Dr. Martin Luther King, Jr., whose "dream" for America was infused with the imagery of liberation from Pharaoh's yoke and a march through the wilderness toward the promised land.[1]

The best way to prepare for this study is to read as much as possible of Exodus 1—24 and the later commentary on the meaning of these events found in Deuteronomy 1—11. Here our primary concern is not with critical details.[2] Rather, we want to enter into the inner meaning of the exodus drama—the meaning which was kept alive and relived in every annual celebration of the Passover feast and in periodic covenant-renewal services at the central sanctuary (Joshua 24). This can be done by concentrating on the passages that have been selected, perhaps with side reference to the sermonic material in Deut. 4:25–40 or 8:1–20. It would be advisable to bypass the question of particular miracle stories for the time being (for example, the plagues) and concentrate on the central miracle of "the mystery of Israel"—the elected people that has survived to this day.

ENCOUNTER WITH GOD

A good place to begin the discussion is with the story of Moses' call in Exodus 3, for this narrative presents the theme of the whole Book of Exodus. Rather than tripping over literal details, read the passage

---

1. See the excellent discussion of Martin Luther King's use of biblical imagery by James H. Smylie in "On Jesus, Pharaohs, and the Chosen People: Martin Luther King as Biblical Interpreter and Humanist," *Interpretation* (1970): 74–91.

2. For a discussion of literary and historical problems, see my *Understanding the Old Testament,* chaps. 1 and 2.

with religious imagination. Perhaps you will find that the dialogue sounds deep notes with which you resonate in your own experience.

Notice that Moses was brought into an I-Thou relation to God not as he was overwhelmed by the grandeur of nature but as he was brooding over the meaning of a historical situation: the plight of his kinsfolk who were crying out under oppression in Egypt. The narrator emphasizes the theme of God's entrance into the human struggle: "I have seen the plight of my people"; "I have heard their cry"; "I know their sorrows"; "I have come down to rescue them." The God of the exodus is not removed from the places where people are struggling and suffering; rather, God is involved, liberating people from bondage and opening a way into the future.

The story of Moses' encounter with God is paralleled in other accounts, like the portrayal of Elijah's contest on Mount Horeb (Sinai) (1 Kings 19), the call of a prophet (see Jer. 1:4–19), a psalmist's awareness of the God who is inescapable (Psalm 139), and the symphony of voices in the New Testament which proclaim that God has spoken and acted in the life, death, and resurrection of Jesus Christ. Therefore, when we speak of revelation we are referring to a personal encounter in which the holy God, who is not a phenomenon of our human world, becomes manifest in the world through word and deed.

Perhaps a human analogy will help to clarify this. We cannot really know any person unless the person discloses herself or himself through speech and action. We can know a lot of things *about* the person, such as family background, education, job, physical appearance, and so on, but we cannot really know him or her in an I-thou relationship apart from self-disclosure in what the person says or does.[3] So it is with God. We cannot know God personally unless God chooses to speak through inspired words and to act with liberating power. Revelation is not receiving ideas about God through some private pipeline of communication; rather, it is God's act of self-disclosure, which results in a new understanding of who we are and of our task in the divine purpose. And this encounter takes place in the concrete situations of human history.

---

3. Some classic discussions of this subject are Martin Buber's *I and Thou* (New York: Charles Scribner's Sons, 1937); his *Eclipse of God* (Harper and Brothers, 1952); and H. Richard Niebuhr's *The Meaning of Revelation* (Macmillan & Co., 1941).

GOD'S PERSONAL NAME

One interesting motif of the Moses story is the giving of God's name. In the ancient world a personal name was not just a label, as it usually is for us, but was closely connected with the person of the bearer. One's name was believed to be a disclosure of one's identity and one's character. Moses, we are told, was reluctant to go back to Egypt because his kinsfolk would surely ask the name of the God who had commissioned him. Moses was given God's name, so the story goes, but only indirectly and evasively—for "I am who I am" is a wordplay on the personal name (Yahweh) which Israelites were to use in worship.[4]

The giving of God's name (that is, God's self) symbolizes God's self-giving, God's self-presentation, to a people. Those who know the name of God know who God is (God's personal identity) and can pray to God in the I-thou relationship of prayer. God is truly present in the midst of the people. But God's name cannot be "taken in vain," that is, used for human purposes, as in some societies even today in which the knowledge of a personal name gives magical power over the bearer. The holy God, who descends voluntarily to the level of the people and identifies with their struggle for liberation, is not subject to human control or manipulation. A close relationship to God does not entitle the people to say that God is "our God" in a possessive sense—the prisoner of their thoughts, social values, or national ambitions. God reserves the freedom to act in surprising ways: "I will be gracious to whom I will be gracious, and will show mercy on whom I will show mercy" (Exod. 33:19). God keeps the initiative.

The prophets of Israel helped the people understand what it means to say, "God is with us" (Hebrew: *immanuel;* cf. Isa. 7:1-17). It means to seek good and not evil and to establish justice (Amos 5:14-15). It means to realize that God's saving action includes the "strange work" of divine judgment upon God's own people (Isa. 28:21-22). It means to experience the "new thing" of God's grace and forgiveness, which makes possible a new beginning (Isa. 43:16-21). The God whom Israel

---

4. In the Revised Standard Version and other modern translations (except the Jerusalem Bible) the sacred name is translated "the Lord," following synagogue practice. For a clear and profound discussion of the giving of God's name, see Gerhard von Rad, *Moses,* World Christian Books (New York: Association Press, 1960), 18–25.

knows and worships is the God who does surprising things which demand a reconsideration of past beliefs, reevaluation of old standards, reinterpretation of previous tradition. And perhaps the greatest surprise of all comes with the New Testament announcement that Jesus of Nazareth is Immanuel, "God with us" (Matt. 2:23). Indeed, according to the Gospel of John, his mission is to manifest God's "name" (nature) to the disciples (John 17:6).

THE COVENANT COMMITMENT

The next three passages (Exod. 19:3–6; 20:1–17; 24:3–8) should be considered together, for they deal with Israel's response to God's intervention on its behalf. Here we come upon the central motif of the biblical drama: the Covenant (Old Testament really means "Old Covenant"; New Testament, "New Covenant"). As in the case of the marriage covenant, this biblical covenant is a personal relationship based on commitment and trust. Unlike the marriage covenant, however, it is more unilateral in character, for it is a covenant between unequals—God and people. It is God who "makes" or "gives" the covenant; Israel responds in gratitude, reverence, and loyalty.

Much light has been shed upon the nature of the Mosaic covenant from ancient treaties or covenants which governed the relations between peoples during the period before David. Among the archives of the ancient Hittites (a people who ruled in Asia Minor, which is modern Turkey, from 1600 to 1200 B.C.) archaeologists have found copies of treaties between the Hittite suzerain and vassal states. The treaty form includes several major elements. To begin with, the "great king" announces his name and titles and declares the benevolent deeds he has performed in behalf of the vassal state. There follows a list of stipulations, including the prohibition of entering into foreign alliances, which are binding upon the vassal in gratitude for favors received. Then, for the vassal who takes the oath of loyalty, these legal stipulations are sanctioned by the invocation of blessing and curse—blessing for obedience and curse (judgment) for betrayal of the covenant. The treaty form also includes a provision for periodic public reading of the covenant laws and the renewal of the vows of allegiance.[5]

---

5. An admirable, nontechnical discussion of the Mosaic covenant in the light of ancient political treaties is found in Delbert Hillers's *Covenant: The History of a Biblical Idea.*

In many respects the covenant between God and Israel is similar to this ancient covenant form, showing that Israel used a prevalent literary vehicle to confess her faith in the God who claimed this people in the event of the exodus. Israel, however, put a new picture into the old frame. The following points deserve consideration:

1. God takes the initiative in establishing the covenant relationship. God enters into the historical situation in an act of self-giving (disclosure of the name) and in acts of benevolence toward a people in distress. Israel does not first choose but is *chosen*. Therefore, faith is wholehearted response to God's initiative as manifested in the "mighty act" which liberates a people from bondage and opens a way into the future.

2. This relationship puts people under an absolute demand: "Thou shalt," "Thou shalt not." In the Decalogue God addresses the people with categorical imperatives, and they are responsible before God in all the relationships of life. One cannot serve God with half one's heart and some other loyalty with the other half. Like any absolute commitment, the covenant allegiance is essentially a "jealous" one. In this connection, read the Shema ("Hear") found in Deut. 6:4–5, which is the central creed of Judaism to this day.

3. The covenant involves not only obligations toward God but obligations toward the other members of the community. This is the meaning of the giving of the law in connection with the making of the covenant. The legal stipulations are adapted to new cultural circumstances, but the basic principle remains constant: persons are absolutely responsible to one another because they are absolutely responsible to God.

4. Ethical responsibility is motivated by gratitude for *what God has done*—for the acts of benevolence manifested in the event of the exodus. Notice the preface to the Ten Commandments: "I am the Lord [Yahweh] your God, who brought you out of the land of Egypt, out of the house of bondage." Israelites are to obey God not as slaves driven to their duties but as a liberated people who stand in awe and gratitude before the gracious deeds of their Redeemer.

5. The Mosaic covenant contains a conditional element: "*If* you will obey my voice and keep my covenant . . ." (Exod. 19:3–6). Faithfulness to the covenant yields blessing; betrayal brings the curse of divine judgment. This element of the covenant was picked up later by the great prophets of Israel.

CHOSEN FOR SERVICE

It is important to see how the exodus story ties in with the dramatic sequence of the Book of Genesis. As we saw in the last study, Genesis 1—3 gives a word picture of the fundamental human situation: the estrangement of humanity from God in spite of its supreme position as God's representative on earth. The consequences of the human tragedy are spelled out in the stories of Genesis 4—11, in which things go from bad to worse. Then we are told in Genesis 12:1-3 that God, to meet this universal human predicament, took appropriate action by calling a man (Abraham) and promising him that his people would be the means of blessing to all the broken and divided families of humankind. The God who speaks to Moses is "the God of the ancestors"—that is, Abraham, Isaac, and Jacob, and Sarah, Rebekah, Leah and Rachel. Thus the deliverance of the Israelites from Egyptian bondage is seen in the perspective of God's redemptive concern to bring all people to the full measure of humanity intended in the creation.

Questions to Think About

1. Some religions (for example, Hinduism) maintain that Ultimate Reality is unnameable; attempts to name God reduce the divine to the level of human distinctions or domesticate the divine in the realm of change and decay. Against this view, how would you understand the story of the giving of God's name to Moses and the people?

2. Does it make sense in our time to say that "God acts in history"? Do you think that Exodus 3:7-8 describes God's involvement with oppressed and exploited peoples today?

3. A justice of the Supreme Court defended a decision by saying that in modern society "there are no absolutes." How does a "situational ethic" square with the covenant faith? Would you say that the Ten Commandments are absolutely binding in every situation?

4. "Thou shalt have no other gods before me." What does God's "jealousy" mean in our situation? What are some of the "gods" that people worship today?

5. A fundamental premise of the Bible, both Old and New Testaments, is that God has "chosen" a people for service. According to your present understanding, discuss the meaning of the election of Israel (or the church).

Suggestions for Further Reading

Anderson, Bernhard W. *Understanding the Old Testament,* chaps. 1 and 2.
Childs, Brevard. *The Book of Exodus.* Old Testament Library. Philadel-

phia: Westminster Press, 1974. A fresh study which stresses the place of the Book of Exodus in the biblical canon.

Clements, Ronald E. *Exodus*. Cambridge Commentary on the New English Bible. Cambridge: Cambridge University Press, 1972. Very helpful.

Croatto, J. Severino. *Exodus: A Hermeneutics of Freedom*. Translated by Salvator Attanasio. Maryknoll, N.Y.: Orbis Books, 1981. A superb example of Latin American liberation theology.

Fackenheim, Emil L. *God's Presence in History: Jewish Affirmations and Philosophical Reflections*. New York: Harper & Row, 1970. A profound discussion of exodus and Sinai in Jewish tradition.

Harrelson, Walter. *The Ten Commandments and Human Rights*. Overtures to Biblical Theology. Philadelphia: Fortress Press, 1980.

Hillers, Delbert R. *Covenant: The History of a Biblical Idea*. Baltimore: Johns Hopkins Press, 1969. A clearly written, illuminating discussion.

Mendenhall, George E. "Covenant." In *The Interpreter's Dictionary of the Bible*. Nashville: Abingdon Press, 1962.

―――. *Law and Covenant in Israel and the Ancient Near East*. Pittsburgh: Biblical Colloquim, 1955. A pioneering study of Israel's covenant tradition in the light of Hittite parallels.

The Discipline
of Disaster

Study Passages

1. Jeremiah 1:4–19
   Appointed to Be a Messenger
2. Jeremiah 2:1–13
   Covenant Lawsuit againt Israel
3. Jeremiah 7:1–15
   The Temple as a Den of Thieves
4. Jeremiah 31:31–34
   The New Covenant

This is a study in tragedy. During Jeremiah's long career as a prophet in Jerusalem (626–587 B.C.), events moved swiftly and inexorably toward the precipice of disaster. The very foundations shook under the shattering impact of ominous historical events. And finally the curtain of the first main act of the biblical drama came down on a scene of utter ruin: the Temple was destroyed, the nation had fallen, and the cream of the population had been carried away into foreign exile. "By the waters of Babylon, there we sat down and wept, when we remembered Zion [Jerusalem]," lamented a psalmist (Ps. 137:1).

THE PEOPLE THAT WALKED
IN DARKNESS

To appreciate the full pathos of the tragedy let us telescope Israel's history from the Exodus to the fall of the nation into a short summary.

After the miraculous deliverance from Egypt the Israelites were forged into a community in the experiences of the desert, where despite their murmurings they repeatedly experienced the grace and the faithfulness of God (Exodus 16—18; Numbers 10—36). With a sense of God-given destiny, kept alive through the memory of the saving event of the Exodus and the covenant of Sinai, they moved into the Promised Land. There, under the leadership of Joshua and his successors, they successfully maintained a foothold despite enemy pressure. For some generations the people were bound together in a tribal confederacy known as Israel. During this period (the two centuries before David) the people came together periodically on occasions of worship to renew their covenantal allegiance to the God who had shown benevolent power in the Exodus. As on the occasion of the great convocation at Shechem under Joshua (Joshua 24), they heard anew the marvelous story of what God had done, they listened to the public reading of the stipulations of the covenant, and they renewed their vow to serve the God of the Exodus and to obey the covenant laws. The formula of Exod. 24:7 was echoed in these services of covenant renewal: "All that the Lord has spoken we will do, and we will be obedient."

In time the community Israel became a nation, and under the leadership of David rose to a height of prestige and glory. In some circles this new development was regarded as the continuation and outcome of what God had started to do in the period of the Exodus. Royal theologians advanced the view that God had entered into a special covenant with Israel *through David* the king, a covenant which guaranteed social stability and the continuity of the Davidic dynasty ((2 Samuel 7). The story of God's saving actions, begun in the Exodus, was seen to point toward the special choice of David and of the temple on Mount Zion in the divine purpose (see Psalm 78, especially verses 67-72). In other words God was continuing to lead the people into the future.

Troubles soon broke out, however. Under the oppressive reign of David's son Solomon there was great restiveness beneath the surface of the nation's glory, and at his death the volcano of revolution erupted. The once-united kingdom was split into North and South by civil strife, the former clinging to the Mosaic tradition and the latter emphasizing the covenant with David. The people of Israel, torn apart by fratricidal rivalry and warfare, were soon caught in the power struggle of the ancient Near East. Crushed beneath the heel of the conqueror, the Northern Kingdom was destroyed by the Assyrians in 722 B.C., and the

Southern Kingdom was finished off by the Babylonians in the fateful year of 587 B.C.

THE CONTEMPORANEITY OF
THE COVENANT

During this tumultuous period there appeared a remarkable succession of prophets—individuals like Samuel, Elijah, Amos, Hosea, Isaiah, Jeremiah, and Ezekiel. In all ancient history there was nothing that matched the succession of prophets who arose in Israel. Today many people suppose that a prophet is a clairvoyant who peers into a crystal ball, as it were, and discloses the shape of things to come. This, however, is a caricature of prophecy.

The true prophet was one who interpreted the meaning of the historical crisis in the light of Israel's covenant loyalty. The prophets were not extremists who introduced radically new conceptions which broke with the past, nor were they reactionaries who merely repeated the old traditions in a new time. Rather, they spoke to the urgent and imperative present of the community by reinterpreting the meaning of the covenant traditions in the present crisis and by warning the people of the consequences of their action for the future.[1]

The tense that matters most in Israel's faith is the present, the *today* of the covenant. This contemporaneous note, frequently heard on occasions of worship in the Israelite community ("O that today you would hearken to his voice," Ps. 95:7) is sounded in a passage in Deuteronomy which serves as an introduction in the Decalogue:

> The Lord our God made a covenant with us in
> Horeb [Sinai].
> Not with our ancestors did the Lord make this cove-
> nant, but with us, who are all of us here alive
> this day.
> (Deut. 5:2–3)

If the prophets speak to us today, it is because in our time the present

---

1. See the discussion of prophecy in my *The Eighth Century Prophets: Amos, Hosea, Isaiah, Micah,* chap. 2, "The Shock of God's Future." See also the discussion of the prophet Hosea by Walter Brueggemann, in *Tradition for Crisis* (Richmond: John Knox Press, 1968). Brueggemann points out that the prophets reinterpreted the old traditions to make them relevant to the present. Incidentally, there are many close affinities between the prophet Hosea, of the north, and Jeremiah, who prophesied in the south about a century later.

is qualitatively the same even though the date is in the twentieth century.

THE TRIAL OF ISRAEL

For this study we have arbitrarily selected Jeremiah as representative of the prophetic movement, and a few passages from the Book of Jeremiah as representative of this prophet's message.[2] During his career (about 626–587 B.C.) Jeremiah saw the colossal Assyrian empire disintegrate. He witnessed the intense nationalism of the Southern Kingdom, fanned by the patriotic hope for independence. He beheld the new Babylonian empire rise from the ashes of Assyria and spread destruction throughout Palestine. What was the meaning of these events? Like prophets who preceded him (for instance, Hosea in the middle of the eighth century B.C.), Jeremiah insisted that disaster was a form of discipline—that is, God was "teaching" the people through these tragic events (as the word "discipline" literally suggests). God was actively confronting the people on the plane of history, leading them through suffering to a new beginning in divine grace. Therefore, even though there was tragedy, it was meaningful tragedy.

The selected passages form a good sequence for discussion. The first one (Jer. 1:4–19) describes Jeremiah's commission in a dialogue which reminds us of the account of Moses' call. The prophet understands himself to be a messenger who is summoned and sent, who speaks not his own opinions but the message of his Lord. Hence the frequent messenger formula "Thus saith the Lord" (see Gen. 32:3–5 for the secular use of the messenger form of speech). Verse 10 is important. Notice that the first effect of God's Word, spoken through the prophetic messenger, is destructive; it "roots up and pulls down." Only after this negative or critical function has been performed does it "build and plant." This calls our attention to a characteristic emphasis of the prophetic message: to know God, or rather to be known by God, is to be exposed to divine judgment. God sets a plumb line against the unjust structures of society (Amos 7:7–9) and searches the innermost motives of the heart (Ps. 139:1–6). There is no dark corner where the searchlight of God's criticism does not reach.

---

2. For a full discussion of Jeremiah and his times, see my *Understanding the Old Testament,* chap. 11. See also my forthcoming *Jeremiah: Prophet of the New Covenant.*

The second passage (Jer. 2:1–13), which contains the message of the prophetic messenger (note the messenger formula in 2:1–2 and 2:4–5a), belongs to a literary genre known as the "covenant lawsuit."[3] The prophet, acting as a prosecuting lawyer who represents God's court, reviews the history of Israel in the light of the covenant commitment. Viewed from this standpoint it is a long history of ingratitude and unfaithfulness to the God who has graciously delivered the people from bondage and brought them into a good land. The past is reviewed not for its own sake but to understand the meaning of the present. The people preferred to live on their own terms, following the idols of their own hearts. The indictment comes to a resounding climax in verse 13, where the prophet accuses the people of rejecting the God who is "the fountain of living waters," to hew out for themselves "broken cisterns that can hold no water." This is reminiscent of the theme we have met previously in the Paradise story.

The third passage strikes at the very heart of the popular belief, encouraged by royal-covenant theology, that the temple is the sign of God's presence with the people. Jeremiah's "temple sermon," which Jesus later referred to (Mark 11:17), is a hard-hitting criticism of religion—that is, of the kind of religion which is the tool of the status quo or "establishment" and the justification of accepted social values or priorities. The prophet warns worshipers against supposing that they are safe if they "go to church" while their society violates the human dignity of persons and thereby shouts defiance at the sovereignty of God. The temple is not a cave where robbers can find refuge to count their spoil! Notice the "ifs" of the conditional Mosaic covenant (verses 5–7) and the specific citation of some of the commandments of the Decalogue (verses 8–10). The blessings of the covenant sanction a life style that shows fidelity to God's demands, but the curses (judgments) of the covenant come inescapably upon a false way of life. The ancient shrine of the old tribal confederacy, once located at Shiloh (1 Sam. 1:3), had been destroyed without trace by the Philistines, and, says Jeremiah, a similar fate will befall the proud temple of Jerusalem. For God is the critic, not the defender, of an unjust social order. On the basis of the covenant, God enters into controversy with the people.

---

3. The covenant lawsuit is indicated by the Hebrew verb in verse 9 translated "contend." This literary genre is discussed by Delbert Hillers, in *Covenant: The History of a Biblical Idea* (Johns Hopkins Press, 1969), chap. 6.

JUDGMENT IN HISTORY

In his time Jeremiah perceived that the historical crisis disclosed the judgment of God, and he summoned people to repent, or amend their way of life, while there was still time. Indeed, he insisted that God was using the Babylonian invader to shock the people to their senses so that they might turn from pursuing the "devices and desires of their own hearts"—to use the words of a familiar prayer—and find the true peace and security of covenant relationship with God. In some respects, Jeremiah's message was like that of Isaiah, who in the latter part of the eighth century B.C. boldly described the Assyrian foe as the "rod of the Lord's anger" which was being used to discipline a rebellious people (Isa. 10:5–19).[4]

It comes down to this. People are free to choose their course of action, but they are not free to escape the consequences of that action as long as God is actively present "with us" in judgment and in mercy. The God for whom the prophets of Israel speak is the Holy One who acts to overthrow systems of exploitation, to humble the proud and exalt those of low degree, and to shatter the false gods (loyalties, values) in which people place their trust. There is, according to the Cambridge historian Herbert Butterfield, a discernible element of judgment in human history.[5] But the end of this shock treatment is that human beings may be brought to their senses, may become more fully human in their relationships, and at last may find their true community in a new covenant with God. This is the theme of the final study passage (Jer. 31:31–34), from which the New Testament takes its name.[6]

Questions to Think About

1. Karl Marx observed that the beginning of all criticism is the criticism of religion. Jeremiah, though speaking from the standpoint of faith in God, would have agreed. Why?

---

4. During the period of Nazi ascendancy in Europe, Harry Emerson Fosdick delivered a hard-hitting sermon on the text from Isaiah, under the title "God Talks to a Dictator." See *Living under Tension: Sermons on Christianity Today* (New York: Harper & Brothers, 1941), 172–81.

5. Herbert Butterfield, *Christianity and History* (New York: Charles Scribner's Sons, 1950).

6. See my exposition of this passage, "The New Covenant and the Old," in *The Old Testament and Christian Faith* (New York: Harper & Row, 1963), 225–42.

2. Make a list of some of the "broken cisterns" (cf. Jer. 2:13) in which moderns have placed their trust. Would you include education, science, psychology, progress, communism, the "American way," organized religion?

3. In his Second Inaugural, Abraham Lincoln said, "If God will that [the Civil War] continue until every drop of blood drawn by the taskmaster's lash shall be repaid with two drawn by the sword . . . then . . . 'the judgments of the Lord are true and righteous altogether.' " Does our present historical crisis disclose the judgment of God? How should this view affect our attitude as citizens?

4. Discuss the widely held view that religion belongs in one sphere and political and economic issues in another. Would Jeremiah have agreed with the policy of keeping social issues out of the pulpit?

5. Jeremiah believed that God was working through an unbeliever, Nebuchadnezzar, to accomplish the divine purpose in history. What do you think Jeremiah's attitude would have been today toward the atheistic rulers of the Kremlin? Toward radical secular forces of revolution in our society?

6. Suppose that Western civilization should fall, as the Roman Empire collapsed in the time of Augustine. How would a biblical prophet interpret this disaster?

Suggestions for Further Reading

Anderson, Bernhard W. *The Eighth Century Prophets: Amos, Hosea, Isaiah, Micah.* Philadelphia: Fortress Press, 1978.

———. *Jeremiah: Prophet of the New Covenant.* Philadelphia: Fortress Press, forthcoming.

———. *Understanding the Old Testament,* chaps. 8, 9, and 10. These chapters discuss in detail the prophetic movement in ancient Israel.

Bright, John. *Jeremiah.* Anchor Bible. Garden City, N.Y.: Doubleday & Co., 1965. A fresh translation with helpful introduction and notes.

Brueggemann, Walter. *The Prophetic Imagination.* Philadelphia: Fortress Press, 1973.

Habel, Norman. *Jeremiah and Lamentations.* Concordia Commentary. St. Louis: Concordia Publishing House, 1968.

Heschel, Abraham Joshua. *The Prophets.* New York: Harper & Row, 1963. A discerning work by a Jewish philosopher.

Holladay, William A. *Jeremiah.* Hermeneia. Philadelphia: Westminster Press, 1987.

———. *Jeremiah: Spokesman Out of Time.* Philadelphia: United Church Press, 1974.

Rad, Gerhard von. *The Message of the Prophets.* New York: Harper & Row, 1965.

STUDY IV

The New Exodus

Study Passages

1. Isaiah 40:1–11
   A Herald of Good News
2. Isaiah 42:5–17; 43:14–21
   The Divine Surprise
3. Isaiah 52:12—53:13
   The Suffering Servant
4. Isaiah 55:1–13
   Promises of the Everlasting Covenant

We come now to the second main phase of the biblical drama. The scene opens in Babylonia, to which country Judahites or Jews[1] had been deported during the capture of the city of Jerusalem. Many of these displaced persons had settled down in relative prosperity and security in the foreign land, but the vision of Jerusalem, destroyed and impoverished, could not be erased from their memories (see Psalm 137). To them the terrible thing was not just the physical calamity but the religious despair and disillusionment which the fall of Jerusalem had occasioned. Jerusalem was not an ordinary city to them. It was a

---

1. While "Israel" refers to the whole people of God, "the Jews" originally designated the residents of Judah, the Southern Kingdom—that is, Judahites—who were exiled from the land of Judah. "Samaritans," on the other hand, were the former citizens of Samaria, the Northern Kingdom, who previously had been exiled by the Assyrians.

center of historical meaning—meaning which had been disclosed when God delivered the Israelites from Egypt and providentially guided their history to its greatest fulfillment in the establishment of the dynasty of David.

A SPIRITUAL BLACKOUT

The crisis of the fall of Jerusalem was experienced intensely by the people of the Southern Kingdom (Judah) who shared the covenant theology associated with King David (see STUDY III). Southern interpreters maintained that the climax of Israel's sacred history was God's choice of David to be king, and of the temple of Zion (Jerusalem) to be God's "dwelling place" (Psalms 78; 132). It was their conviction that God made an "everlasting covenant" with David and his line (Psalm 89) and set aside Jerusalem with its temple as the "city of God" (Psalms 46; 84). This theological view provided a guarantee of social stability amid the disorders of history, when every change of administration was an opportunity for disruptive, chaotic forces to break loose.[2] Yet the poignant question inevitably arose: If God had made unbreakable promises of grace to David and had designated Jerusalem as the central place of worship, why did God allow a terrible calamity to occur which brought the Davidic line to an end and destroyed the temple? The anguish of this question, raised in a time of national distress, is vividly expressed in Psalm 89, particularly in the lament with which it concludes (verses 38–51).

The fall of Jerusalem was thus a spiritual blackout, especially for those who identified God's purpose in history with the preservation of the Davidic state. Jeremiah 28 provides a vivid description of the tension between nationalism and faith, between popular prophecy and true prophecy. The popular prophet had declared, "God is with us" (the meaning of the Hebrew word *immanuel*), therefore no evil can come upon us. The genuine prophet had said, "God is with us," therefore all securities—Jerusalem, the Temple, organized religion, the nation—stand under divine judgment. It is easy to see how those who had been beguiled by popular prophecy would have concluded that God had "let them down" when Jerusalem was destroyed. It seemed that the whole history of God's covenant with Israel was a history of failure!

---

2. See my discussion of the theology of social stability represented by the Davidic covenant, "Creation and Covenant," in *Creation versus Chaos.*

But the God who in the past led a dispirited band of slaves out of Egypt was about to open a way into the future once again. This is the testimony of a series of magnificent poems found in the latter part of the Book of Isaiah (chapters 40–55). Speaking to despairing exiles in Babylonia, this prophet announces the good news that the God of Israel, who controls the destinies of all nations, will accomplish the return of the Israelites to their homeland, where they will take their part in the fulfillment of the divine purpose for history. Strikingly, this prophet resorts to the imagery of the exodus from Egypt to describe Israel's new "going out" from captivity and the opening of a new way into the future (Isa. 44:27; 43:16–17; 51:10–11; compare Exod. 14:15–31). It is appropriate, then, to speak of this event as the "New Exodus."[3]

THE ECUMENICAL PURPOSE
OF GOD

It is generally recognized that the last part of our present Book of Isaiah, particularly chapters 40–55, comes from a follower of the eighth-century prophet, who about two centuries later, in the time of the exile, reinterpreted the message of his master. Usually the "unknown prophet of the exile" is called Second Isaiah to distinguish him from Isaiah of Jerusalem (740–700 B.C.), whose prophecies are found in the first section of the Book of Isaiah (chapters 1—39).

In the time of Second Isaiah the Babylonian empire was declining, and the political news on the international scene was the rise of a ruler named Cyrus (Isa. 44:28; 45:1). Having established control over the Medes and the Persians (about 550 B.C.), Cyrus marched into the heart of the Babylonian empire, and in 538 Babylon fell. Second Isaiah was active in the period between the rise of the new conqueror and the final capitulation of Babylon—that is, between 550 and 538 B.C. An enlightened monarch, Cyrus granted captive peoples the right to live in their own countries and to carry on their own traditions. Small wonder that many people who groaned under the heavy yoke of Babylonia looked to him as a messianic liberator! This is the life situation to which the "unknown prophet" spoke. His task as a prophetic messenger was not

---

3. I have discussed at greater length the motif of the "new exodus" in "Exodus Typology in Second Isaiah," in *Israel's Prophetic Heritage*, 177–95.

just to predict the imminent downfall of Babylon and the release of cap-
tives but to interpret the religious meaning of this momentous event.

The best way to prepare for this study is to read through all fifteen
chapters of Second Isaiah (Isaiah 40–55) in a modern translation. From
a purely literary point of view this is poetry at its finest. From a theological viewpoint these poems represent the crowning maturity of the
faith of Israel. The passages selected set forth themes which are elaborated with symphonic splendor in the prophet's work as a whole. The
central thrust of the prophetic message is that world events do not
happen by caprice but are embraced within the overruling sovereignty
of God, the Creator and Redeemer, to whom Israel's historical traditions bear witness.

A HERALD OF GOOD NEWS

Like a prologue, the first passage (Isa. 40:1–11) sets the tone of the
whole series of poems. The prophet (who appears in the "I" of verse
6) senses that he has stood, as it were, within the Heavenly Council
where God was heard issuing a decree to be announced to Israel—and
to the whole world. A key word in this section is "good news" (verse
9; compare 52:7), the word which reappears in the New Testament as
"gospel." What is the content of this good news? It is this: God is about
to act, just as at the beginning of Israel's history God took the initiative
to deliver a people from a no-exit situation and to open a way through
the wilderness into a promised future. To an unbeliever, perhaps, there
would be nothing extraordinary in the return of exiles to their homeland. But to those who viewed this event in the perspective of the
Exodus and the whole Israelite tradition, this would be a theophany—a
manifestation of the glory of God on the stage of history:

> Behold, the Lord God comes with might,
>   and his arm rules for him. . . .
> He will feed his flock like a shepherd,
>   he will gather the lambs in his arms,
> he will carry them in his bosom,
>   and gently lead those that are with young.
>   (Isa. 40:10–11; compare 52:7–10)

In the prophet's ecstatic faith, the historical drama was moving toward
the dawn of the New Age, the kingdom of God. It is significant that

at the beginning of the third stage of the biblical drama John the Baptist recapitulates the theme of this chapter (compare Isa. 40:3 with Mark 1:3).

One of the central themes of the prophet's message is the *novelty* of God's action in history (Isa. 42:5–17; 43:14–21). Life is not merely lived within the order of nature with its recurring rhythms of "seedtime and harvest, cold and heat, summer and winter, day and night" (Gen. 8:22) but is caught up in a purposive movement of historical events that are new, unique, and unrepeatable. The nations, when brought to trial, are unable to testify to this divine purpose in which the startling developments under Cyrus are related to the "former things" (the call of Abraham, the Exodus from Egypt, the march through the wilderness to the Promised Land). But Israel, out of her own life story, bears witness to the God whose purpose spans the ages, from beginning to end.

At times the prophet seems to stress the newness of God's action so sharply that the past is to be forgotten:

> Remember not the former things,
>   nor consider the things of old,
> Behold, I am doing a new thing;
>   now it springs forth, do you not perceive it?
>   (Isa. 43:18–19)

Yet the prophet is equally insistent that Israel should "remember the former things of old" (Isa. 46:8–11). These statements are not contradictory when one considers the creative manner in which the prophet reinterprets the old traditions so that they are convincingly relevant to the present situation in which the community finds itself. Here the Israelite tradition is not just a past memory but provides the imagery for understanding the new thing which God is doing, the new word which he is speaking. Again and again the prophet resorts to the tradition of the Exodus from Egypt to describe the New Exodus of salvation. The prophet is not talking, however, about a repetition of the first Exodus. Rather, the imagery of the old is used poetically to express the divine surprise which is about to occur.

THE SERVANT OF THE LORD

According to Second Isaiah, Israel is the Lord's "Servant" (Isa. 41:8–10; 43:8–13; 44:1–2). This Servant is blind, deaf, and stubborn. Still, despite his weaknesses, the Servant has been chosen for a unique role in the accomplishment of God's historical purpose. God had an ulterior motive in delivering Israel from Babylonian bondage: that Israel might be a "light to the nations" (42:6; compare 49:6). Here the prophet understands profoundly the meaning of the call of Abraham and Sarah to be a blessing to the families of the earth (Gen. 12:1-3).

> Look to the rock from which you were hewn,
>   and to the quarry from which you were digged.
> Look to Abraham your father
>   and to Sarah who bore you;
> for when he was but one I called him,
>   and I blessed him and made him many.
>   (Isa. 51:1-2)

This theme is developed with sublime grandeur in our third passage (Isa. 52:12—53:13), which belongs to a series of special "servant poems."[4] In this passage, one of the most important in the whole Old Testament, the "Suffering Servant" is portrayed in the guise of an individual. At the beginning and end of the poem (52:13-15; 53:10-13) God speaks, announcing the exaltation of the Servant. In the central portion (53:1-9) the representatives of the nations testify. They have come to realize that the meaning of Israel's suffering was not merely that the people had experienced the discipline of divine judgment. That was part of the matter, to be sure, but there was a much deeper truth. The Servant's suffering was vicarious—that is, it was borne for others. Through the Servant's affliction the peoples were made whole, restored to health, "justified" or brought into right relationship with God and with one another. This is the most astounding testimony of the Bible: that God chooses the way of humiliation, suffering, rejection, and defeat to make known divine glory and triumph in the world. And this is the truth which is fulfilled and "made flesh" in the New Testament.

THE PROMISES OF GRACE

The final chapter (Isa. 55:1-13) rounds off the prophet's message by sounding again the theme of unconditional pardon and grace heard at

---

4. Besides this chapter, there are three other servant poems: Isa. 42:1-4; 49:1-6; 50:4-9. The identity of the servant in Second Isaiah is a moot question. See my discussion in *Understanding the Old Testament*, 488-500.

the beginning. A free-for-all invitation is given to God's banquet table. Here the startling announcement is made that the unconditional covenant of grace, once made with David according to royal theology (2 Samuel 7), is now extended to *the people* (Isa. 55:3). The covenant relation with God is not based upon obedience to legal stipulations, as in the Mosaic covenant, but is grounded solely upon the grace of God whose thoughts are not our thoughts and whose ways are not our ways. God makes an "everlasting covenant" with the people, like the covenant with Noah whose sign is the bow in the clouds (54:9–10; compare Gen. 9:8–17). This covenant of grace, which is central to the gospel of the New Testament, does not relieve human beings of responsibility. Rather, it provides the motive for turning from evil ways and unworthy thoughts and returning to the God whose mercy is immeasurable and whose ways exceed human comprehension (Isa. 55:6–9).

Questions to Think About

1. Contrast Second Isaiah's understanding of history with the nihilistic view that history has no ultimate meaning and that we must find our temporary meanings. What is the ground for saying that all human history from beginning to end is embraced within a single purpose?

2. How does the prophet's announcement that God is "doing a new thing" speak to our time? Does this demand a break with past tradition and a radically new theology?

3. Compare the Mosaic covenant and its conditional stipulations with the "everlasting covenant" which is grounded solely in divine grace. Do you think that a greater emphasis upon divine grace (pardon, forgiveness) undercuts the motive for human action and responsibility?

4. How does Second Isaiah view the "election" or call of Israel as having a special role in the divine purpose? How do you account for the "mystery of Israel"—the people which has survived through the centuries to the present?

5. Granting that the church is the "new Israel," does it participate with Jesus Christ in the mystery of the Suffering Servant? If so, what does it mean to share the fellowship of Christ's sufferings?

Suggestions for Further Reading

Anderson, Bernhard W. "Exodus Typology in Second Isaiah." In *Israel's Prophetic Heritage,* ed. B. W. Anderson and Walter J. Harrelson. New York: Harper & Row, 1962.

———. *Understanding the Old Testament,* chap. 18.

McKenzie, John L. *Second Isaiah*. Anchor Bible. Garden City, N.Y.:
    Doubleday & Co., 1968. A fresh translation with helpful introduction
    and notes by a Roman Catholic scholar.
Muilenberg, James. "Introduction and Exegesis to Isaiah 40–66." In *Inter-
    preter's Bible*. Nashville: Abingdon Press, 1956. An excellent com-
    mentary.
Westermann, Claus. *Isaiah 40–66.* Old Testament Library. Philadelphia:
    Westminster Press, 1969.

STUDY V

The People of
the Torah

This brings us to one of the most important, though for many Christians the most problematic, phases of the biblical drama. The spotlight falls on Ezra and Nehemiah, two men who played a decisive role in the re-formation of Israel into the community known as Judaism. (The religious phenomenon called Judaism emerged during the period after the exile when "Jews" [former residents of Judah] returned to Palestine. It was characterized by devotion to the Mosaic Torah [the Pentateuch] as the constitutional basis of life and thought.)

Someone has said that Israel went into exile as a nation and returned as a church. The word "Judaism" refers to a new stage in the biblical drama when Israel was no longer a state but a religious community— somewhat analogous to the time before David when the people were united in a tribal confederacy on the basis of covenant allegiance. This worshiping community was an ellipse with two centers: the temple and the Torah.

A NEW BEGINNING

To see this in proper perspective, we need to resume the story from the time of Second Isaiah, practically a century earlier than the period of Ezra. Shortly after Babylon capitulated to the Persian army, Cyrus issued an edict allowing Jews the privilege of returning to their home- land. So Jewish exiles began their homeward trek to Zion (Jerusalem). When they arrived, they found everything in ruins: the temple was destroyed, the walls of Jerusalem were leveled, the city desolate. Nev- ertheless, inspired by the prophecies of Haggai and Zechariah, they set about rebuilding the temple, a project which was completed about 515 B.C.

Then Ezra came onto the scene, according to the sequence of events given by the historian who wrote the Books of Chronicles, Ezra, and Nehemiah. With the permission of the Persian king he led a caravan of Jews back to Palestine around the middle of the fifth century B.C., or slightly later. Most important, he brought with him a copy of "the book of the law [torah] of Moses" (probably the Pentateuch, the so-called Five Books of Moses), and he lost no time in convening the people to hear the reading of its contents. One of the solemn moments in Israel's history is described in Nehemiah 8 and 9, a great occasion of covenant renewal. The ceremony included the public reading of the Torah to the people, the offering of a penitential prayer which summarized the Lord's gracious dealings with the people throughout their historical pil- grimage, and the covenant pledge of the people "to walk in God's law [torah], which was given by Moses the servant of God." The event is to be compared with the covenant-renewal ceremony led by Joshua (Joshua 24) or by King Josiah (2 Kings 23).

At about the same time Nehemiah, a cupbearer to the Persian king, received permission to return to Palestine as a Persian governor of

Judah. After a memorable midnight tour around the city walls of Jerusalem, he organized the Jews for work, and in less than two months the walls were rebuilt, despite hostile resistance. Thus under the religious leadership of Ezra and the statesmanship of Nehemiah the "congregation of Israel" took a new lease on life. It seemed as though the glowing promises spoken by prophets like Second Isaiah were on the verge of fulfillment.[1]

COVENANT RENEWAL

The vitality of Judaism is indicated by the great amount of biblical literature which comes from the period following the exile. The Pentateuch (the first five books of the Old Testament) received its final form in this period. Indeed, the whole Old Testament as we have received it is stamped indelibly with the way of life and thought characteristic of the time. In this study we can do little more than scratch the surface of biblical Judaism, the stage of Israel's historical pilgrimage out of which Christianity emerged in the fullness of time.

The best way to prepare for this study is to familiarize oneself with the account of Ezra's career as it is related in Ezra 7—8; Nehemiah 8—10; Ezra 9—10 (the chapters should be read in that order). In these chapters you will find an emphasis upon ritual, or "priestly," matters, which loom large in long sections of the Pentateuch, as well as a concern for maintaining the purity of the faith by rigid laws against mixed marriages. Above all, attention should be given to the account of Ezra's reading of the Torah (Nehemiah 8:1-8) and the solemn liturgical prayer which followed (Neh. 9:6-38).

Notice that the prayer strikes a note characteristic of Israel's faith from the first. It is a summary of the "mighty acts of the Lord" by which Israel had been brought onto the stage of history with a unique vocation and destiny. Penitently the people acknowledge that the Exile was God's judgment upon their covenant unfaithfulness. Gratefully they rejoice in the New Exodus from Babylonian captivity. Solemnly they vow to renew the covenant by obeying the stipulations of the Torah. This is one of the great confessions of faith in the Old Testament. Unlike Israel's early creedal confession (Deut. 26:5-9), the recital of

---

1. For a discussion of these developments, see my *Understanding the Old Testament,* 507–39.

God's saving acts begins with the creation, as does the "salvation-history" or "storytelling" Psalm 136, which probably comes from this period. We have already found this spacious perspective in the message of Second Isaiah, which was addressed to "the people in whose heart is [God's] law" (Isa. 51:7). And in the portrayal of the Consummation found in Isa. 2:1–5 (Micah 4:1–4) the peoples of the world stream to Jerusalem, from which God's *torah,* or Word, goes forth. Thus the Torah discloses the meaning of all history and creation.

REJOICING IN THE TORAH

Of the great amount of literature from the period of Judaism we have selected for special study some of the psalms of Israel and some of the writings from Israel's wisdom movement. The Book of Psalms is so important in Jewish and Christian worship that it would call for a special study by itself.[2] Like modern hymnbooks, it reflects a long history of worship in which songs of various types are included: hymns of praise (for example, Psalm 103), laments and confessions of sin (Psalms 22; 51), thanksgivings (Psalm 118), and songs for use on special occasions (Psalm 47, a New Year's psalm). The final edition of the Book of Psalms, however, is a product of the period of Judaism and is appropriately arranged in five books like the Pentateuch itself. The hymnbook is introduced with two psalms which set forth the cardinal tenets of Judaism: Psalm 1, which glorifies the study of God's Torah (see also Ps. 19:7–14), and Psalm 2, which in this period, as in the time of the New Testament, was understood to refer to the Messiah (see also Psalm 110). Thus these introductory psalms invite readers "to choose the right path to the Messianic glory: the study of the law and obedience toward the word of God."[3]

So, after becoming familiarized with the Ezra story, turn to Psalm 1. This psalm draws a distinction between two kinds of persons: the "God-fearer" who delights in God's Torah day and night and who therefore is like a tree whose roots are nourished by life-giving waters, and the "wicked" person or the "fool" (Ps. 14:1) who vainly lives by

2. See my *Out of the Depths,* (Philadelphia: Westminster Press, 1983), especially chap. 7.

3. Aage Bentzen, *Introduction to the Old Testament,* 4th ed. (Copenhagen: G. E. C. Gads Vorlag, 1958), 2:170.

self-chosen standards, without dependence upon God. Remember that when the Israelites thought of God's "law," they did not think of a heavenly police officer who coldly enforces statutes. Rather, they confessed their relationship to the God who had graciously redeemed Israel from bondage and had given them "teaching" or "direction" (the proper translation of the Hebrew word *torah*) in the way they should walk. From the very first the covenant and the Torah were linked together. As time went on, many "laws" were added to the covenant tradition, and under Ezra the Torah was identified especially with the Pentateuch, the so-called Five Books of Moses. You would think that obeying the many instructions of this Torah would be burdensome. But reading the Torah psalms (Psalms 1; 19:7–14; 119) will disclose that Judaism found God's Torah a delight, "rejoicing the heart" (Ps. 19:8). For the chief concern was that of glorifying God in all daily actions and relationships.

> Oh, how I love thy law [*torah*]!
>   It is my meditation all the day.
> Thy commandment makes me wiser than my enemies,
>   for it is ever with me.
>
> (Ps. 119:97–98)

THE BEGINNING OF WISDOM

Ezra's great reform had its strengths but also had great dangers which were evident to those who reflected deeply upon the sufferings and imbalances of life. It is one thing to delight in God's will. It is another to be so self-righteously sure of what God's will is in a specific situation that one thanks God that one is not as other people (see the parable of the Pharisee and the publican, Luke 18:9–14). Perhaps modern churches and synagogues fall into this danger insofar as a middle-class code of "thou shalts" and "thou shalt nots" is set forth as the standard of virtue. And leaders who claim that God is on our side in the international struggle imply self-righteously that our enemies are the wicked who fall short of the glory of God. According to Israel's prophets, God's will brought the people under judgment; the Lord had a controversy with Israel. If we think seriously about how impossible it is to stand before God on the basis of moral goodness (Psalm 130:3), perhaps we can anticipate why the Christian gospel protests against all legalism and moralism and puts our relation with God on an entirely different basis from the *torah,* or "law" (Gal. 2:11–21).

The belief of Judaism was that God's Torah is the source of wisdom, as we can see from a wisdom psalm like Psalm 37 (see especially verses 30–31). Wisdom, therefore, is not a human achievement but a gift bestowed by God, one that inspires humility and reverence:

> Behold, the fear of the Lord, that is wisdom;
> and to depart from evil is understanding.
>
> (Job 28:28)

Those who have this sort of faith may reach understanding; those who fail at this starting point are "fools" who grope in ignorance.

THE VOICE FROM THE WHIRLWIND

Some of Israel's sages pushed their search for understanding into the mystery of God's creation and even dared to raise questions about the justice of God's ways. This is the case in the Book of Job, one of the greatest literary contributions of Israel's wisdom movement. The author of this work has been aptly acclaimed the "Shakespeare of the Old Testament."

Ideally, for this study unit the whole Book of Job should be read. But at least read the selected portions recommended at the beginning of this chapter. Notice that an old folk tale, written in prose, now stands as the prologue and epilogue to a poetic work which consists of Job's lament (chapter 3), his conversation with his friends in three rounds (chapters 4—27), his final oath of innocence (chapters 29—31), God's answer out of the whirlwind (chapters 38—41), and Job's repentance (42:1–6; compare 40:1–5). The author has used the old tale as a "framing device," inserting his poetry into this envelope for the purpose of dramatic contrast.[4]

The Job of the story is a traditional righteous person, "blameless and upright, an individual who feared God, and turned away from evil"— one who bears adversity with calm patience and long-suffering. The Job of the poem, however, refuses to suffer the "slings and arrows of

---

4. For further discussion of the Book of Job, see especially Samuel Terrien, *Job, Poet of Existence.* See also my *Understanding the Old Testament,* 588–601.

outrageous fortune" meekly and without protest. Not only does Job challenge his three orthodox friends, who steadfastly insist that his suffering has been brought about by some sin, but also he dares to expostulate with God and even to accuse God of maladministration of justice on earth. Finally, after an overwhelming demonstration of God's wisdom and power as Creator (the Voice from the whirlwind), Job acknowledges that he has no ground on which to challenge the Almighty and repents of his presumptuous speech.

Various questions will come to mind in reading the book. What is the real problem with which Job wrestles? Why can he not accept the "pastoral counseling" of his friends? Is the Voice from the whirlwind an answer to Job's question? Why does Job recant or repent in the end? Having heard the Voice from the whirlwind, what does he mean by the statement "Now my eye sees you"?

However these questions are treated, the poet brings us to an awareness of the great gulf that is fixed between the Creator and the creature. God's wisdom, which grasps the entire scheme of creation, is inaccessible to human beings; God's power that upholds the creation is overwhelming. Perhaps the Book of Job will provide a context for appreciating the message announced at the beginning of the Gospel of John: that the chasm has been bridged, for the Logos (Word) of creation has become flesh (John 1).

Questions to Think About

1. The first Psalm suggests that the person who obeys the will of God will enjoy security, influence, and long life. Discuss the difference between the attitude of this psalm and that of Psalm 73, with its great "nevertheless" in verse 23.

2. What strengths and weaknesses do you see in Ezra's great reform? Discuss what "legalism" means in the church today.

3. The great keynote of Israel's sages was "The fear of the Lord is the beginning of wisdom" (Prov. 9:10; 15:33; Job 28:28; Ps. 111:10). Consider what this means, perhaps by studying the magnificent poem in Job 28.

4. Archibald MacLeish has attempted to interpret the meaning of the Book of Job for our time in his play *J. B.: A Play in Verse* (Boston: Houghton Mifflin, 1961). What aspects of the poem of Job does he ignore? What new dimensions are added?

5. The test of any religion is how it deals with the problem of suffering and evil. How is this problem dealt with in the prophecy represented by

Jeremiah? In Second Isaiah's portrayal of the Suffering Servant? In the Book of Job?

Suggestions for Further Reading

Ackroyd, Peter. *Exile and Restoration: A Study of Hebrew Thought of the Sixth Century B.C.* Philadelphia: Westminster Press, 1968.

Anderson, Bernhard W. *Understanding the Old Testament,* chaps. 15, 16, and 17.

Clines, David J. A. *Ezra, Nehemiah, Esther.* New Century Bible Commentary. Grand Rapids: Wm. B. Eerdmans, 1984.

Kidner, D. *Ezra and Nehemiah: An Introduction and Commentary.* Tyndale Old Testament Commentaries. London: Inter-Varsity Press, 1979.

Wisdom Literature

Crenshaw, James L. *Old Testament Wisdom: An Introduction.* Atlanta: John Knox Press, 1981.

Habel, Norman. *The Book of Job.* Old Testament Library. Philadelphia: Westminster Press, 1985. One of the best commentaries available.

Rad, Gerhard von. *Wisdom in Israel.* Nashville: Abingdon Press, 1973.

Scott, R. B. Y. *The Way of Wisdom in the Old Testament.* New York: Macmillan Co., 1971.

Terrien, Samuel. "Introduction and Exegesis to Job." In *Interpreter's Bible.*

————. *Job: Poet of Existence.* Indianapolis: Bobbs-Merrill, 1958.

The Book of Psalms

Anderson, Bernhard W. *Out of the Depths: The Psalms Speak for Us Today.* Revised edition. Philadelphia: Westminster Press, 1983.

Brueggemann, Walter. *The Message of the Psalms.* Minneapolis: Augsburg Publishing House, 1984.

Weiser, Artur. *The Psalms.* Old Testament Library. Philadelphia: Westminster Press, 1962.

Victory Through Defeat

Study Passages

1. Acts 10:34–43
   To Him the Prophets Bear Witness
2. Mark 8:27—9:13
   Peter's Confession
3. 1 Corinthians 1:17—2:9
   The Scandal of the Cross
4. 2 Corinthians 5:14—6:2
   The New Creation

The historical drama, in which God is the Chief Actor, has now reached its climax. The New Testament opens with the exuberant announcement that God's promises to Israel are being fulfilled. John the Baptist, the last of Israel's prophets before the dawn of the messianic age, appears on the scene in a manner reminiscent of Elijah, announcing that the great consummation (the day of judgment and renewal) is at hand. Jesus of Nazareth steps onto the stage of history at this crucial juncture, and his message is pitched to a key of urgency:

> The time is fulfilled, and the kingdom of God is at hand; repent, and believe in the gospel. (Mark 1:15)

THE CHRISTIAN GOOD NEWS

Earlier we have seen (STUDY IV) that the Christian term "gospel" has its scriptural background in passages of Second Isaiah where the

61

prophet, like a herald, announced the good news of God's coming in triumph to inaugurate a new age (Isa. 52:7-10). Likewise in the New Testament the gospel is the good news that God's redemptive rule (kingdom) has begun, that the new age has dawned. The good news is not a new doctrine, such as the fatherhood of God and human brotherhood (compare Mal. 2:10), but is the announcement of what God does: God delivers humanity from the bondage of evil, darkness, and death, and re-creates human life with new possibilities of freedom and fulfillment. Moreover, the New Testament proclaims that the good news is Jesus himself—his words and works which confront people with the authority of one who is uniquely *anointed* to be God's agent. (The Greek word for Christ [*christos*] is equivalent to the Hebrew word for Messiah [*mashiach*], which means "anointed one"—that is, one who is consecrated as the agent of God's rule.)

Jesus preaches with eschatological urgency: *now* is the time to decide, tomorrow may be too late; for the kingdom of God is at hand! (The word "eschatological" comes from a Greek word *eschata* referring to the "last things"—that is, the end. In this context "end" refers to the great consummation which is so near that it is already beginning to break into history.) Above all, the gospel focuses on the crucifixion and, the other side of this event, the resurrection. If the exodus was a mighty act of God, if the deliverance of Jewish exiles from captivity was a divine deed, then God's greatest miracle in history was what has been called the "Christ event"—the whole life, death, and resurrection of Jesus and the consequent emergence of the church.

The written Gospels (Matthew, Mark, Luke, John) are not biographies in our sense of the word but are primarily confessions of faith, each with a different accent and perspective. This does not mean that the literary Gospels belong in the category of fiction or fantasy, for the gospel story is based securely upon the earthly career of a historical person. Nevertheless, Jesus' words and works were remembered in the experience of those who, after the crucifixion and resurrection, were convinced that he was God's Messiah (Christ)—the anointed one of God (Acts 10:38). Thus in the earliest Gospel, Mark, the focus of interest is chiefly on the passion of Christ. Another formulation of the Christian gospel is found in Peter's sermon as presented in Acts 10:34–43, a passage which you should take time to read, for it presents the basic outline of the Christian story.

THE DENOUEMENT OF THE
HISTORICAL DRAMA

To appreciate the Christian conviction that the Christ Event is the fulfillment and climax of the previous episodes of the biblical drama, let's
take a brief glance back at the story which has unfolded thus far. The
biblical drama begins by describing in pictorial terms humanity's
estrangement from God—the misuse of the freedom God has given and
the resulting confusion, conflict, and chaos in history. To deal with this
general human predicament, God took the initiative—so we are told in
Gen. 12:1-3—and called Abraham, promising him that he and his
descendants would be a blessing to the broken and distraught families
of humankind. So Israel was called and formed as a special community
in order that this people might be the bearer of God's purpose in history, the agent for the accomplishment of God's historical plan. Israel's
record, however, was one of persistent betrayal of the covenant loyalty,
and the catastrophes that struck in the periods of Assyrian and Babylonian world rule were interpreted by prophets as the discipline of God's
judgment. Then, buoyed by the stirring prophecy of Second Isaiah and
the leadership of Ezra and Nehemiah, a fresh start was made after the
Exile. But in the period of Judaism, Israel became so preoccupied with
the problem of preserving its own identity and tradition that the world
mission described by Second Isaiah was almost lost to sight, except for
a few witnesses like the Book of Jonah. At last, in the fullness of time
(Gal. 4:4), Jesus of Nazareth appeared in the context of the history of
God's people.

> Then came, at a predetermined moment, a moment in time and of
>   time,
> A moment not out of time, but in time, in what we call history;
>   transecting, bisecting the world of time, a moment in time but not
>   like a moment of time,
> A moment in time but time was made through that moment;
>   for without the meaning there is no time, and that moment of time
>   gave the meaning.[1]

Thus the Christian church affirms that in this "moment of time,"
which divides history into B.C. and A.D., God has made a new begin-

---

1. T. S. Eliot, from "Choruses from 'the Rock,' " VII, in *Collected Poems 1909–
1962* (Harcourt, Brace and Co., 1963), 199. Used by permission.

ning, has introduced the New Age in which people may begin to experience a richer and fuller humanity. Through Christ, the Church proclaims, a new life is available: a new relation to God and, as a corollary, a new relation between human beings. Jeremiah's prophecy of the New Covenant (see STUDY III) took on deeper meaning for Christians who appropriated the scriptural tradition. The Christian community, like the monastic community which flourished at Qumran on the shore of the Dead Sea,[2] understood itself to be the community of the new covenant. When the shadow of the Cross fell upon the table at the Last Supper, Jesus said to his disciples, "This cup is the new covenant in my blood" (1 Cor. 11:25; compare Luke 22:20), recalling both the ceremony at Sinai (Exod. 24:3–8) and Jeremiah's prophecy (Jer. 31:31–34).

THE NEW CHRISTIAN LANGUAGE

The Christian community, however, did not merely repeat the tradition of the past but used it creatively to declare what God is doing now. Perhaps the major characteristic of this community was the new language that it used to tell the Christian gospel. The "narrative mode," Amos Wilder points out, "is uniquely important to Christianity," unlike other religions and philosophies in which the telling of a story is relatively peripheral. Like any good drama, the Christian story has a powerful quality which involves its hearers, questions their existence, and draws them into the narrative. In the story of Christ's passion, for example, there are many episodes involving everyday persons, such as the maid in the courtyard of the high priest (Mark 14:66–70) and Simon of Cyrene, who was compelled to bear the cross of Jesus (Mark 15:21). Rather than permitting us to stand at a distance, these minor anecdotes make the Christian story one with which we can identify. As Wilder observes,

---

2. The Essene community of Qumran thought of itself as the eschatological community of the new covenant. More can be found out about this community by turning to Miller Burrows, *The Dead Sea Scrolls* (Grand Rapids: Baker Book House, 1978); Joseph A. Fitzmyer, "Scrolls, The Dead Sea," in *Harper's Bible Dictionary,* 915–17; and G. Vermes, "Dead Sea Scrolls," in *Interpreter's Dictionary of the Bible,* supplementary volume, 210–19.

Perhaps the special character of the stories of the New Testament lies in the fact that they are not told for themselves, that they are not only about other people, but they are always about us. They locate us in the very midst of the great story and plot of all time and space, and therefore relate us to the great dramatist and storyteller, God.[3]

WHO DO YOU SAY THAT I AM?

Within this dramatic context we should read the story of Peter's confession at Caesarea-Philippi and its sequel, the story of the Transfiguration (Mark 8:27—9:13). Since this is the turning point in Mark's passion story, the best preparation would be to read the whole Gospel through, sensitive to the role of minor characters in the drama.[4] The recurring question is, Who is this Stranger who speaks with authority, who performs the deeds which evidence God's active presence in the world, who is rejected by the religious authorities and misunderstood by his own followers, and who finally goes his lonely way to the cross? "Who do *you* say that I am?" Neutrality is out of the question; decision is demanded.

Notice that the mystery of Jesus' identity was heightened by his announcement to his disciples that his vocation was that of the Suffering Servant and that those who follow after him would share his suffering. Strangely, he *must* suffer (Mark 8:31–33). Why this divine necessity? In those days it was generally believed that the Messiah would come triumphantly to restore the lost fortunes of Israel, either by political action or supernatural power, and achieve thereby a victory that would be clear to all. How incredible that Second Isaiah's portrayal of the Suffering Servant, which the prophet apparently applied to the sufferings of Israel (see STUDY IV), could be a depiction of the role of the triumphant Messiah!

The story of the Transfiguration (Mark 9:2–13) connects the Crucifixion-Resurrection with the previous episodes of the biblical drama. In Israelite tradition the appearance of a prophet "like Moses"

---

3. Amos Wilder, *The Language of the Gospel,* 64–65.

4. On the "little people" in Mark's Gospel, see Donald Michie and David Rhoads, *Mark as Story: An Introduction to the Narrative of a Gospel* (Philadelphia: Fortress Press, 1982), 129–35.

(Deut. 18:15-16) or another Elijah (Mal. 4:5) would mark the time of the End, the coming of God's kingdom. It is significant, then, that in the disciples' vision these two figures, Moses and Elijah, appear in company with Jesus. In a kind of religious ecstasy the disciples perceive the splendid uniqueness of Jesus; but the sequel of Mark's story shows that they could not really understand the divine victory that lay on the other side of the cross. Their continuing lack of faith is a commentary on Jesus' rebuke to Peter for being not on the side of God but of human beings (Mark 8:33).

THE SCANDAL OF THE CROSS

The theme of the mystery of the Cross is treated at greater length in a letter Paul addressed to the church at the Greek city of Corinth (1 Cor. 1:17—2:13). Here Paul points out that to the nonbeliever, whether Jew or Gentile, the cross is either foolishness or an offense, stumbling block (*skandalon*). If the Christian gospel were only the preaching of a loftier ethic or the belief in a Supreme Being the world would have little difficulty with this faith. But the trouble is that Christians proclaim the wisdom of God in what the world considers foolishness, and the power of God in what the world regards as weakness and defeat. Take away the Cross, Paul testifies, and there is no gospel to proclaim. The Cross is the distinctive Christian symbol of God's victory in apparent defeat.

Some may think it strange that we do not focus our attention first on Jesus' teachings as found in the Sermon on the Mount (Matthew 5—7). The reason for this is that the early Christians did not start there. *They began, rather, with a recital of the story of Jesus—his Passion and his Resurrection.* Teachings and ethical exhortations had their proper place *after* one was drawn into the believing community. The good news was not an ethical code or a new religious idea. It was, rather, the telling of the marvelous story that in Jesus of Nazareth, God had actively entered into the human struggle, changing Jesus' suffering and defeat into victory by raising him from the dead and inaugurating a "new creation." Paul discusses the momentous results of God's action in another communication to the church at Corinth which deserves careful study (2 Cor. 5:14—6:2). There he announces the triumphant theme that "God was in Christ reconciling the world" to God's self (2 Cor.

5:19)—overcoming the sin which finds expression in our separation from God, from one another, and from our true selves, and restoring us to the unity and dignity which God intends for the creation.

Questions to Think About

1. The custom of dividing the Western calendar into B.C. and A.D. goes back to the sixth century, when a monk named Dionysius Exiguus attempted to calculate the date of the birth of Christ. Today many are using the more neutral designations B.C.E. (Before the Common Era) and C.E. (Common Era). What is at stake in this discussion about the calendar?

2. Viewed in the light of the New Testament, how is Jesus' death different from the martyrdom of Socrates, Abraham Lincoln, Mohandas Gandhi, or Martin Luther King, Jr.? Why was the Cross "necessary" to the accomplishment of God's purpose for mankind?

3. Evaluate the popular view that the essence of Christianity is the Golden Rule or the Sermon on the Mount. What is the "new" that has been introduced through God's action in Jesus Christ?

4. The historian Arnold Toynbee once said that the Transfiguration is the key to the Christian interpretation of history. Does it make sense to affirm that the hidden meaning of world history is disclosed in Jesus Christ?

5. Why is the Cross a "scandal" (offense, stumbling block) to many modern people? Have you become familiar with this "scandalous cross" or are you more familiar with a watered-down Christianity? Discuss the "costs" of Christian discipleship.

Suggestions for Further Reading

Achtemeier, Paul J. *Mark.* Proclamation Commentaries. 2d revised edition. Philadelphia: Fortress Press, 1986.

Kee, Howard. *The Community of the New Age: Studies in Mark's Gospel.* Philadelphia: Westminster Press, 1977. An illuminating treatment of Mark's Gospel in the light of apocalyptic tradition.

———. *Understanding the New Testament.* 4th edition. Englewood Cliffs, N.J.: Prentice-Hall, 1984.

Minear, Paul. *The Gospel according to Mark.* Layman's Bible Commentaries. Richmond: John Knox Press, 1962. Clear, concise introduction.

Perrin, Norman. *The New Testament: An Introduction,* chap. 8. 2d edition. Revised by D. Daling. New York: Harcourt Brace Jovanovich, 1982.

Wilder, Amos. *The Language of the Gospel.* New York: Harper & Row, 1964. A clearly written, incisive contribution to the understanding of the New Testament.

The Church in
the World

Study Passages

1. Romans 9—11
   The Israel of God
2. Peter 2:4–10
   The Rejected Stone as the Cornerstone
3. Ephesians 1:3—2:22
   The Church in God's Universal Design
4. John 17
   That They May Be One

In this study our attention focuses on a new emergent in history: the church of Jesus Christ. From the very first, Christianity was characterized by an esprit de corps, a sense of membership in a corporate reality which Paul called the body of Christ (1 Cor. 12:27). The individualism which characterizes some modern expressions of Christianity is completely foreign to the New Testament, so much so that the phrase "individual Christian" is a contradiction in terms. The various churches at Antioch, Jerusalem, Ephesus, Corinth, and elsewhere were local manifestations of the corporate whole, the Body. Jesus himself conceived his mission to be that of calling the remnant of Israel—twelve disciples, corresponding to the twelve-tribe structure of Israel. And when the meaning of Jesus' life, death, and resurrection came upon these disciples with overwhelming power at the festival of Pentecost (Acts 2), one of the major annual festivals of the Israelite calendar, a great miracle occurred. This small community became a dynamic and militant church, with a message that "turned the world upside down" (Acts 17:6) and a gospel that was carried enthusiastically to the ends of the earth. The Acts of the Apostles gives the story of the emerging, expanding church. And every line of the New Testament presupposes the new community.

THE ISRAEL OF GOD

While stressing the newness of the Church, we must also keep in mind the relation of this community to the whole Old Testament heritage. In a certain sense the Church may be called the New Israel. The Old Testament narrates how a people was formed to be the bearer of God's purpose in history and the instrument of God's saving work. Israel was not a race or a nation but a covenant community created by God's action (Exod. 15:16b; Ps. 100:3; Isa. 43:15; 44:2). Having delivered Israel from the miserable lot of slavery in Egypt, God made them a covenant people. Through many tumultuous years God educated and disciplined them in order that they might understand more deeply the meaning of their special role in history. It was Second Isaiah who understood most profoundly Israel's place in God's worldwide purpose. According to the prophet's interpretation, Israel was called to be a "light to the nations" and a servant whose sufferings would benefit all humankind. However, in the period of Judaism, as we have seen, these spacious horizons were obscured. Jewish devotion to the Torah had the effect of sharpening the division between Jew and non-Jew and even separated Jews from their close relatives, the Samaritans (see John 4:7–30, especially verse 9: "For Jews have no dealings with Samaritans"). The last two centuries before Christ witnessed a resurgence of Jewish nationalism which led in time to the Jewish wars with Rome. This story is told in part in 1 Maccabees—a book that belongs to the Old Testament in expanded form (Apocrypha). In A.D. 70, under the emperor Titus, the Romans destroyed the Temple, leveled Jerusalem, and removed the last vestiges of Jewish statehood. (See the depiction on the Arch of Titus in Rome today.)

So, in the fullness of time God acted once again to reconstitute the community of Israel—no longer bound by the ethnic or nationalistic limitations of Judaism but open to all people, whether Jew or Gentile, on the basis of faith. The new community does not establish a clean break with the people of God whose life story is portrayed in the Old Testament; rather, it is—as Paul puts it in his important discussion in Romans 9—11—a "remnant chosen by grace." It is, so to speak, a "wild olive shoot" grafted into the olive tree (Israel); and the "branch" is supported by the roots which reach down deeply into the biblical story of God's choice of Israel and God's faithful dealings with this people (Rom. 11:17-24). The whole passage deserves thoughtful study, for it casts light upon the affinity between the Jewish and Christian communities, which cannot be effaced by differences over the identity of the Messiah.

THE CORNERSTONE OF THE
FOUNDATION

Of the many passages in the New Testament which deal with the calling and mission of the new community, three have been selected for special study. You will find that each deals with an important characteristic of the Church. The first of these (1 Pet. 2:4-10) brings the accent down upon the truth that this "pilgrim people" has been established by God's action through Jesus Christ, the "living stone" who is the foundation of a "spiritual house." The Church is not essentially a social organization or a human institution which can be understood by sociological analysis; it is, rather, a creation of the Divine Architect who has chosen the rejected Stone (Jesus Christ) as the foundation. This imagery harks back to a passage in Psalm 118, a royal thanksgiving which celebrates God's gracious acts in history.[1] In this psalm—Martin Luther's favorite—the key passage is verses 21-24, especially the jubilant cry that the Stone which the builders would have rejected as poor material has become the cornerstone of the foundation (compare Isa. 28:16). The Stone referred to is the remnant of Israel—a "well-tested stone" upon which God would build. According to our passage in 1 Peter, the remnant is reduced to one—to Jesus Christ, the foundation of the Church. Notice that the expressions in verse 9 previously had been applied to the chosen people at the time of the making of the Covenant (see Exod. 19:4-6); now they are applied to the New Israel which was

---

1. On this and related psalms, see chap. 4 of *Out of the Depths*, especially 82-87.

once "no people" (compare Hos. 2:23) but which in the grace of God
has become "God's people":

> But you are a chosen race, a royal priesthood, a holy nation, God's
> own people, that you may declare the wonderful deeds of him who
> called you out of darkness into his marvelous light. Once you were
> no people but now you are God's people; once you had not received
> mercy but now you have received mercy. (1 Pet. 2:9–10)

THE CHURCH IN GOD'S
WORLD PURPOSE

The place of the Church in the movement of God's purpose for the
world, from Creation to Consummation, is developed with symphonic
splendor in the Epistle to the Ephesians (Eph. 1:1–14; 3:8–12). This
epistle is such an eloquent summary of the Christian gospel in Pauline
terms that it would be profitable to take a few minutes to read it
through.[2] Notice that the Church is described in terms of two main
images: first, the image of the temple of which Jesus Christ is the chief
cornerstone (2:19–22), and second, the distinctively Pauline image of
the Body of which the Head is Christ who coordinates all the parts
(1:22–23; 4:15–16; compare Col. 1:18–19).

Perhaps it would be well to concentrate attention on chapter 2 of
Ephesians, where the fundamental theme of the new life and harmoni-
ous unity of the church is sounded, a theme which is elaborated in the
second part of the epistle (chapters 4—6). Here it is appropriate to look
into the biblical meaning of the word "peace" (Greek: *eirēnē;* Hebrew:
shālôm). We usually think of peace as the absence of war, but in the
Bible peace has a more positive meaning. Peace is a state of harmony,
wholeness, and welfare within the community. And it is a basic biblical
premise that there cannot be right relations within the community
unless human beings are in right relation with God, for when separated
from God people are at odds with themselves and with one another.

---

2. Some scholars believe that Ephesians is "deutero-Pauline," that is, written by
a disciple whose thinking was closely akin to Paul's. The words "at Ephesus" are
lacking in Eph. 1:1 in the best manuscripts. The tone of the letter is quite general,
without reference to local conditions at Ephesus in Asia Minor (modern Turkey).
Others hold that this is a general letter which Paul intended for reading in a number
of churches in Asia Minor.

The Jewish philosopher Martin Buber has observed,

> The true community does not arise through people's having feelings for one another (though indeed not without it), but through, first, their taking their stand in living mutual relation with the living Centre, and second, their being in living mutual relation with one another.[3]

Thus the commandment about loving God comes first and supplies the basis for loving the neighbor (Luke 10:25–37).

As Old Testament prophets looked away from the broken and fractured society of Israel, they anticipated the coming of the age of the Messiah, when the barriers of separation would be overcome and human beings would be brought into a new relation with God and hence with one another and even with the natural environment (Isa. 11:1–9). Thus in Ephesians love is not a commandment but a new reality in human relationships which has been initiated by the prior manifestation of God's love through Jesus Christ. The most deep-seated antagonism of the time—the separating wall between Jew and Gentile—has been broken down and human beings are reconciled "in one body through the cross." The Church is a fellowship of love—the highest endowment of God's Spirit (see 1 Corinthians 13; 1 John 4:7–12).

JESUS' PRAYER FOR THE CHURCH

The theme of the unity and fruitfulness of the Church in the world is elaborated in Jesus' so-called high-priestly prayer in John 17. Jesus has completed his mission, which is to reveal God's "name" (see STUDY II) to his disciples, the nucleus of the Church. In his final prayer, two prepositions are important: "out of" and "into." God has summoned a people for Christ "out of" the world (verse 6). Indeed, the New Testament word for church (*ekklesia*) literally means "called out," and suggests the conception of God calling people out of the world into a new and unique fellowship. But the Church is not taken out of the world— the secular sphere—into a sheltered and detached life; rather, it is sent "into" the world (verses 15, 18). If the Church is not *a part of* the world, it is also not *apart from* the world. Rather, it is God's task force,

---

3. Martin Buber, *I and Thou* (New York: Charles Scribner's Sons, 1937), 45.

God's mission in the world. The Church has inherited the vocation of the Servant described by Second Isaiah: to be a light to the nations and to be the instrument of God's healing the broken relationships of society.

Above all, Jesus' prayer is for the unity of the Church—"that they may be one, even as we are one" (verses 11, 22). The close relation between Christ and God in the Spirit is to be manifest in the corporate unity and harmony of the Church. And this unity is to be the most convincing demonstration to the world that Jesus has been sent by God as the Way, the Truth, and the Life.

Questions to Think About

1. How does Paul deal with the "mystery of Israel" in Romans 9—11? What implication does this passage have for Jewish-Christian relations today?

2. In the Bible the Church is described by various images: flock, vine, building, pilgrim people, body, and so on. What is the intention of each of these images? Which is most meaningful for our time?

3. Does the breaking-down of the "wall of separation" between Jew and Gentile have any implications for other racial and social problems facing the Church today?

4. What is the relation between the Church and the many "churches" of our time? Does the unity of the Church lie in organization? If not, what is the basis of the unity expressed in the familiar hymn "Elect from every nation, yet one o'er all the earth"?

5. What does it mean in our time for the Church to be a mission in the world? What should the Christian's attitude be toward secular expression in art, literature, movies, folk rock, social action, and so on? On the relevance of modern literature, see, for instance, Cleanth Brooks, *The Hidden God* (New Haven: Yale University Press, 1963).

Suggestions for Further Reading

Barrett, C. K. *A Commentary on the Epistle to the Romans.* Harper's New Testament Commentaries. New York: Harper and Brothers, 1957. An excellent commentary on Paul's most important letter.

———. *Reading through Romans.* London: SCM Press, 1977. A more popular yet discerning treatment.

Beker, J. Christiaan. *Paul the Apostle: The Triumph of God in Life and Thought.* Philadelphia: Fortress Press, 1980. An understanding of Paul as heavily influenced by apocalyptic theology.

————. *Paul's Apocalyptic Gospel: The Coming Triumph of God.* Philadelphia: Fortress Press, 1982.

————. *Suffering and Hope: The Biblical Vision and the Human Predicament.* Philadelphia: Fortress Press, 1987.

Best, Ernest. *One Body in Christ: A Study of the Relationships of the Church in the Epistles of the Apostle Paul.* London: SPCK, 1955.

Minear, Paul. *Images of the Church in the New Testament.* Philadelphia: Westminster Press, 1960. Especially helpful for this study unit.

Sanders, James A. "Torah and Christ," in *From Sacred Story to Sacred Text* (Philadelphia: Fortress Press, 1987), 41–60. Reprinted from *Interpretation* 29 (1973): 372–90. An illuminating treatment of Christ as "God's climactic act" in the biblical story.

Epilogue: In the End

Study Passages

1. Revelation 21:1–8
   A New Heaven and a New Earth
2. Revelation 21:22—22:5
   The New Jerusalem
3. 1 Corinthians 15 (especially 15:12-23, 51-58)
   The Resurrection of the Body
4. Romans 8:18-39
   More Than Conquerors

Like any drama, the biblical drama has a beginning, a climax or denouement, and an end. This elementary observation is exceedingly important for the understanding of the biblical view of history. Unlike the ancient Greek historians who believed that history moves in circles, and unlike some modern historians who believe that the historical process is a phase of the growth and decay of nature, the Bible affirms that our lives are part of a great drama that moves in the direction of a goal. The opening words of the Bible, "In the beginning God . . . ," are matched by the expectation that "in the end" God's purpose will be realized (1 Cor. 15:24-28). All things—history and nature, heaven and earth—are caught up in the purpose of the God who is the First and the Last, the Alpha and the Omega. Therefore, telling the time is not just a chronological reckoning by clocks and calendars; it is the ability to know the content of the times (Ecclesiastes 3) and to discern that, as a psalmist put it, our times are in God's hand (Ps. 31:15), embraced within the divine sovereign purpose.

THE HORIZONS OF HISTORY

It has been observed that when it comes to the interpretation of human history there are, in general, three possible views: (1) history is meaningless flux from which the religious person seeks escape (Hinduism, Buddhism); (2) history secretes its own meaning in the course of cultural evolution (Progress, Marxism); and (3) the hidden meaning of history is made known by God who, as Creator, transcends the whole finite world of sensory experience. The biblical view is that the meaning of the historical drama has its source in the Creator who comprehends the beginning and the end, who surveys and participates in the drama in its entirety, and who, according to Christian conviction, has set forth the mystery of God's will in Jesus Christ as a "plan" which unites all things, earthly and cosmic (Eph. 1:9–10).

In the first study unit we considered the prologue to the biblical drama of God's action in history. Now we turn our attention to the epilogue. It should be obvious that we cannot speak of either the first things or the last things except in the language of relegous symbolism. In both cases we are dealing with ultimates which lie beyond the range of our finite knowledge, beyond our immediate historical experience. Therefore we must speak in the language of faith—faith which rests not upon our ability to fathom or to chart the beginning and the end but upon the meaning that has been disclosed in the unique historical tradition beginning with the Exodus and culminating in the Christ Event. In the vision of Christian faith human history as we know it is bounded by Beginning and End, two horizons which recede into the vistas of God's eternity.

PARADISE REGAINED

A good place to begin the discussion is with the portrayal of the New Heaven and the New Earth found in the last book of the New Testament, the Revelation (or Apocalypse) of Saint John the Divine. This is an exceedingly difficult book to understand because it is written in a code which cannot be deciphered without some knowledge of the persecution of the Church at the time (about A.D. 90) and the genre of literature known as "apocalyptic."[1] Much confusion has been wrought by people who have read the book as though they were gazing into a crystal ball, supposing that some mysterious blueprint for the future is hidden in it. We have tried to facilitate the study by selecting two brief passages (Rev. 21:1–8; 21:22—22:5) in which the symbolism is not quite so obtuse. Even so, there are references which will not mean much without the help of a good commentary. For instance, "The Sea was no more" (21:1) is an allusion to the mythical Great Deep, the locus of rebellious powers which God has held in check since the time of Creation.[2] In other words, this is not the drying-up of water but the overcoming of the powers of evil that menace God's creation. (Herman Melville's novel *Moby Dick* makes effective use of the biblical sea symbolism.) And the Lamb, of course, is the triumphant Christ (see John 1:29).

Two things are especially noteworthy about these passages. First, the portrayal of the New Heaven and the New Earth (compare Isa. 65:17–25) gathers up some of the symbols of the Paradise Story, such as the Tree of Life. Thus the end of the biblical drama recapitulates the beginning: the New Creation corresponds to the First Creation. Second, the consummation of history is symbolized under the figure of the New Jerusalem, the City of God, descending from heaven. In previous studies we have found that Jerusalem in biblical tradition was more than an ordinary city. Jerusalem meant much more to the Israelite than Athens to the ancient Greek or Washington, D.C., to a present-day American. According to the "urban theology" developed in Davidic circles, Jerusalem was the City of God, the place consecrated by God's presence among the people. Indeed, Jerusalem was identified with the mythical mountain of God at the center ("navel") of the earth, from which sprang a river fed by life-giving waters from the great deep (Ps. 46:4; Ezek. 47:1–12). Medieval maps which pinpointed Jerusalem as the center of the universe were based on bad geography and astronomy.

---

1. The word "apocalyptic" comes from the word "apocalypse," which means "revelation" to a seer. The best example of this type of literature in the Old Testament is the Book of Daniel, likewise written in a time of persecution (about 165 B.C.). See further my *Understanding the Old Testament*, 618–33.

2. The "sea" or "chaos" imagery is discussed at length in my *Creation versus Chaos*. See especially chaps. 4 and 5.

But they expressed an important religious conviction. In the perspective of Christian faith, Jerusalem stands for the rule of God in the center of the world, as in Augustine's classical work *The City of God* or in Haydn's hymn "Glorious things of thee are spoken, Zion, city of our God." In the Apocalypse of John the bold claim is made that history ultimately will fulfill and complete the meaning represented by Jerusalem: all nations will find their peace and unity by walking in the light of the new Jerusalem (Rev. 21:24–26; compare Isa. 2:1–4).

Thus the Bible begins with a vision of Paradise Lost and concludes with a vision of Paradise Regained. In between this prologue and this epilogue unfolds the drama of God's entrance into the human struggle to win back the lost creation and to restore humanity to peace, unity, and fullness of life. God's strategy involves the choice and discipline of a people, and finally the way of the Cross. But the end of God's redemptive activity is the final conquest of evil, death, darkness, and all powers which corrupt and threaten the creation. The Church lives by this hope, and prays and strives for the coming of God's kingdom.

THE DECISIVE BATTLE IS WON!

This brings us to the third passage, a portion of 1 Corinthians 15. The background of this passage is the apocalyptic view, expressed in Dan. 12:2–3 and Isa. 26:19, of the final Consummation (the Last Judgment), when the dead will be raised up in order that the faithful may share in the conclusion of the historical drama.[3] In much of the chapter Paul argues that the "body" that will be raised is not the physical body but a *spiritual* body, surpassing the present form of our bodily existence. It is worth noting, in passing, that the body is considered to be the expression of the *person* in the wholeness of the person's personality, the unique self who finds life in relation to other persons and to God. Don't stumble over the literal details. Paul's intention is to affirm that the individual is *given* a future by the God who is gracious and faithful,

---

3. The biblical hope for a future life is not expressed in the Greek doctrine of the immortality of the soul, which presupposes a deathless element imprisoned in the body, but in the apocalyptic category of resurrection of the person. For an interpretation of the words of the Apostles' Creed "I believe in the resurrection of the body," see Reinhold Niebuhr, *Beyond Tragedy* (New York: Charles Scribner's Sons, 1938).

although exactly how this is to occur, says Paul, is "a mystery" (1 Cor. 15:51).

The important thing to notice in this passage is that God's victory over evil, darkness, and death has already occurred—even before the End which is described pictorially in the Revelation of John as "a new heaven and a new earth." Of this the Christian has already been given assurance through the resurrection of Christ, for his victory constitutes the "first fruits" which give promise that the harvest is coming (1 Cor. 15:20). Or, as Paul puts it elsewhere, through Christ's resurrection we have been given the Spirit as an "earnest" or guarantee of what is to come (2 Cor. 1:22; 5:5)

This means that the center of gravity in the Christian gospel is not a longing for a consummation yet to come. The distinctive note of the New Testament is the announcement that the Messiah, the Christ, has already come to inaugurate his kingdom. Already he has won the decisive victory, and therefore through him humanity may taste *now* the life of the new age, "eternal life." A New Testament scholar, Oscar Cullmann, has expressed the relation between the "already" and the "not yet" in a figure of speech drawn from political experience. In some wars of the past the decisive battle occurred at an early stage of the campaign (for instance, the Battle of Britain during the Second World War). Although the struggle continued until the end of the war, the issue had already been decided. Cullmann uses this as an analogy to express the Christian conviction that the "earnest" or "down payment" of God's ultimate triumph has been given in the life, death, and resurrection of Jesus Christ, even though the historical struggle continues for an indefinite time until the outcome is evident to all.[4] In other words, the Christian gospel is a call to action in a contest whose final victory has *already* been won. Members of the Christian community who share this conviction live in the hope that ultimately God's kingdom *will* come in fullness and that "God will be everything to everyone" (1 Cor. 15:28).

It is significant, then, that Paul ends his discussion of the body of the

---

4. Oscar Cullmann, *Christ and Time* (Philadelphia: Westminster Press, 1950), 81–93. He observes, "That which has already happened offers the solid guarantee for that which will take place. The hope of the final victory is so much the more vivid because of the unshakably firm conviction that the battle that decides the victory has already taken place" (p. 87).

resurrection not with speculation about the life beyond the grave but with an appeal for action and responsibility (note the "therefore" of 1 Cor. 15:58). There is a profound this-worldliness in the New Testament gospel, especially when it is read in the context of the whole biblical drama. The ultimate horizon of the consummation, when all tears will be wiped away and there will be no more mourning or suffering, is intended as an endorsement of the fundamental goodness of life as we now experience it. The Christian gospel is not a utopian promise that human beings can achieve the good society through their own planning and efforts; nor is it the promise of release from the changes and transience of mortal existence, as in some Hellenistic cults of the New Testament period. Rather, it announces that none of our work is in vain because it is embraced within the purpose and love of God manifested in the midst of human history through Jesus Christ.

This is the theme to which Paul returns in the last and major letter that he wrote: the epistle to the church at Rome (Rom. 8:18–19). Paul looks squarely at the sufferings of the present age, the tremendous odds that are arrayed against the realization of God's purpose. He is more impressed, however, with the victory *already* won and the opportunity to share in the power of that victory in the present. The motive for action and responsibility is the confidence that all our human successes and failures, our joys and sorrows, are embraced within the triumphant purpose of God. "In everything," writes Paul, "God works for good with those who love him" (Rom. 8:28). Thus, though the trials and conflicts of history are not yet concluded, the believing community lives in the assurance that "in all these things we are more than conquerors through him who loved us" (Rom. 8:37).

Questions to Think About

1. What dramatic effect is achieved in the Bible by placing the historical drama between the horizons of Beginning and End? Compare this portrayal with other views of human existence, such as the Buddhist, the humanist, the communist, and the nihilist.

2. Is it proper to identify the kingdom of God with the better world which human beings hope to achieve through social planning or revolutionary action? Is the kingdom of God a social ideal?

3. Does it make sense to say that the New Age has already been inaugurated through the life, death, and resurrection of Jesus Christ, even before

the final Consummation? What changes has this dawn of the Kingdom made in human life?

4. How does the Christian's "ultimate hope" affect or motivate one's political and social responsibilities in the present historical order? What are some of the "proximate hopes" that we may expect to realize?

5. Traditionally, Christianity has preferred to express belief in the future life in terms of the resurrection of the body rather than in terms of the dualistic doctrine of the immortality (deathlessness) of the soul. Comment on the difference between these two ways of expression. Why is the former more appropriate for the confession of Christian faith, as in the Apostles' Creed?

Suggestions for Further Reading

Caird, G. B. *A Commentary on the Revelation of Saint John the Divine.* Harper's New Testament Commentary. New York: Harper & Row, 1966.

Kubler-Ross, Elisabeth. *Death: The Final Stage of Growth.* New York: Simon and Schuster, Touchstone Books, 1986.

Küng, Hans. *On Being a Christian,* 356–61. New York: Doubleday & Co., 1976. A good discussion of the hope of resurrection.

Minear, Paul S. *I Saw a New Earth: An Introduction to the Visions of the Apocalypse.* Washington, D.C.: Corpus Publications, 1968. This book will reward study.

Russell, D. S. *The Method and Message of Jewish Apocalyptic.* Old Testament Library. Philadelphia: Westminster Press, 1965. A reliable survey of apocalyptic literature from 200 B.C. to A.D. 100.

Schüssler Fiorenza, Elisabeth. *The Book of Revelation—Justice and Judgment.* Philadelphia: Fortress Press, 1985.

Suggestions for
Bible Study Leaders

PURPOSE

Those who plan to set up a Bible study group should have at the outset some understanding of the uniqueness of the venture. This is not a literary circle devoted to the study of one of the great books. The uniqueness of a Bible study group lies in that which is at the center: *the Bible.* The Bible continues to exert a strange power over people's lives because it searchingly exposes the human situation in the light of God's Word spoken in human words, and finally made flesh in Jesus Christ. It deals with our human story and God's involvement in it. Since all of us are inescapably involved in human existence with its glory and complexity and tragedy, there should be a place in the group for any concerned person. Those with Christian convictions (and probably they will be in the majority) will find in the Bible a deeper understanding of the relevance of biblical faith to personal life and world history. Skeptics who are sincerely seeking for light on the meaning of human existence may discover that in some respects the Bible speaks to their condition. But all members of the group will have a common purpose: to hear what the language of the Bible says to us in our life situation today.

The key word for Bible study is "encounter." What takes place in the group is personal encounter with one another and with the God who speaks to us through the Bible. This distinguishes Bible study from the kind of classroom study in which our primary relation is to a body of knowledge rather than to persons. However, the personal encounter of a Bible study group is not that of a glorified bull session in which discussion is carried on in an argumentative spirit, usually without any common frame of reference. In this case the conversation has a common center, a common frame of reference. There will be disagreements, for we each approach the Bible out of our private and cultural background, which usually means with a great deal of ignorance and even rebellion. It is the testimony of the ages, however, that God speaks to us as persons when we listen to the language of the Bible receptively, expectantly, honestly. Often this means that the presuppositions of the questions we bring to the Bible are challenged; often it means the realization that we have not asked the basic question; often it means being disturbed and changed at the very center of our being. But this is what we must expect if we risk an encounter with God. The Trappist monk Thomas Merton hit the nail on the head:

> It is of the very nature of the Bible to affront, perplex and astonish the human mind. Hence the reader who opens the Bible must be prepared for disorientation, confusion, incomprehension, perhaps outrage.[1]

LEADERSHIP

Who should be the leader? This is a difficult question. Some groups have effectively used the principle of rotation—that is, each time, a different member of the group is responsible for the meeting. Often this runs against the snag that some members are not yet far enough along in their understanding of the Bible. And if the blind lead the blind, probably everyone will fall into the ditch! Other groups have found that it is better to rely on a leader who is more mature in biblical understanding (this may be a theological student, a staff leader, a professor, or a minister). No rule of thumb can be given, since groups vary so much.

Qualities of good leadership. The main task of the leader is to help the group go to the heart of the biblical passage, so that there may be a genuine encounter with the Bible rather than a mere rearranging of prejudices. This means that the leader should have some ability in

---

1. Merton, *Opening the Bible*, 11.

group discussion and should have a fairly good knowledge of the Bible (though not necessarily that of an expert). The good leader is one who brings the discussion back to the biblical passage when it wanders astray, who patiently guides the discussion so that disagreements are fruitful, who encourages others to participate in the conversation, and who helps the group to go deeper than answers which merely scratch the surface and to avoid hasty rejection of what some may think they have outgrown. Above all, the leader is the servant of the group and should encourage the rest to have a sense of responsibility for the preparation and participation which will make the study a vital group experience.

Preparation. It cannot be emphasized too strongly that this is a *study* group in the best sense of the word. Therefore the success of the group is dependent upon disciplined and serious preparation on the part of all members. At the minimum, this preparation must be the careful reading and pondering of the selected biblical passages with the aid of the study guide. This applies especially to the leader. Careful study of the material will enable the leader to discern what is central and what is peripheral in the group discussion. Also, the leader should be acquainted with the necessary background material for understanding the passages, turning whenever possible for guidance to the "Suggestions for Further Reading" at the end of the introductory section and each study unit and the "General Suggestions for Further Reading" at the end of the present section. It never hurts to reread the text again and again, and in its broader context. A passage in Mark, for instance, may become clearer in the total context of the full Gospel of Mark.

Resource persons. Often study groups include a "resource person" (a minister, teacher, staff member) who can be consulted when information is needed on a particular point. It is important to find the kind of person who is both congenial and who will not "lord it over the group" with his or her contributions. Frequently, however, such knowledgeable persons tend to lean over backward on this matter—that is, they are so afraid of dominating the discussion that they do not speak until spoken to. Somehow this should be worked out so that the resource person is truly and fully a member of the group—on a level of equality with other participants rather than being set up on a pedestal because of her or his superior knowledge. Perhaps it would be well to forget about the idea of a resource person and think rather of team leadership, in which a novice and an experienced person cooperate in preparing for the meeting and guiding the discussion.

PROCEDURE IN THE
GROUP SESSION

First of all, help the members of the group to feel at home with one another. In a classroom you can get by without knowing who is sitting next to you, for your concern is the mastery of a body of knowledge, not a relation between persons. Bible study, however—as we have said—is a relation with persons by means of the spoken word, and an encounter with God whose Word is mediated through human words. Since the Word of God establishes personal relationship rather than communicating a body of facts, the rapport of interpersonal relationship in the group is essential.

At some point in this informal opening the leader should begin the discussion of the selected biblical passage(s). In some situations it might be appropriate to have a brief prayer or a few moments of silence. The important thing, however, is that the entire Bible study be carried on in a serious and reverent spirit.

It should be kept in mind, above all, that Bible study is an *interaction* between the text and the readers, between the Bible and the situation in which we find ourselves.[2] This premise of group discussion has two interrelated aspects:

1. The primary task is to understand what the biblical writer intended to say. This may involve such questions as, Who was the author? When was the text written? What was the historical and cultural setting? To whom was the writing addressed?

2. Closely related to this is the question about what the text means *for us* in our historical and cultural situation. This calls for an exercise of imagination, like that of actors who put themselves into the script of a play. Remember that "the letter kills, it is the Spirit that gives life." The Bible should not be treated as a soothsayer's manual which gives us literal, specific directives on everything under the sun. It may be that

---

2. See my *The Living Word of the Bible,* especially 34–35.

there are some places in the Bible where, as someone has said, God does not say anything to us except perhaps, Go, read a commentary.

Accordingly, the leader may begin by giving whatever brief background is necessary for the study of the selected biblical passage. Perhaps on subsequent occasions the leader could ask other members of the group to do this in order that the group as a whole may sense a shared responsibility. After this brief introduction of the passage, or perhaps before, it would be well to ask the group to read through the passage—or some portion of it—silently. The more everyone has read the selected texts ahead of time, the more familiar they will be with the message of the text; and the results of the study session are likely to be more rewarding. Or it may be decided to ask someone to read the passage, or a small unit of it, aloud. Many of our selected texts have an oral quality to them (the Psalms, for example). If there are difficult words, they should be explained. *It is important to turn to another translation of the passage for additional light.*

Sometimes groups have found it helpful to begin the discussion by attempting to paraphrase the passage in terms of our own modern language—that is, "put it in your own words." This is a good discipline, for it demands (1) coming to terms with what the original writers meant to say, and (2) interpreting their intentions in our own categories. This may occasion the interaction between the Bible and our situation which, as we have said, is the very essence of Bible study. Moreover, this gets away from the false idea of private interpretation of the Bible. *We do not have the right to make the Bible say what we think it ought to say.* We must discover what the original writer meant to say and translate that meaning into the experiences of our time. Group conversation around the Bible, guided by the Holy Spirit, will lead to a deeper understanding of biblical truth. Don't be afraid to raise "unorthodox" questions, for these may help to sharpen the issues and God may use the skeptic to lead us into new truth. On the other hand, don't be afraid of "orthodoxy"—only try to "beat the crust back into the batter" of Christian experience. The questions included in the study guide at the end of each unit may help initiate and focus the discussion.

The discussion should move according to blocks of Scripture which the leader has isolated in his or her private preparation. When she senses that it is time to move on, she may give a summary of a given unit of material. Above all, the leader should not be anxious about the discussion, as though its success were dependent upon keeping it going. Don't be troubled when there are periods of silence. Don't try to hurry the group along because of the feeling that a given amount of material has to be covered; it is better to stay with a passage until the group is ready to move on. Don't answer important questions impatiently; it may be better for the group to come to the answer on its own. Or perhaps the question should be left open or held over until the next gathering. The leader's purpose is not to lead the group to conclusions foreseen during the preparation; rather, let the conclusion come out of the dialectic of the discussion.

CLOSING THE SESSION

Close on time if possible. The leader may signal the end of the discussion by giving a brief summary and showing the relation of the discussion to the previous study session or to studies that follow. It may be appropriate to follow the summary with a brief prayer, such as the words found in Ps. 139:23–24.

Keep in mind that the foregoing remarks are only general suggestions. No plan should be superimposed inflexibly upon a Bible study group.

General Suggestions for
Further Reading

Orientation

Consult some of my writings, such as "The Dramatic Movement of Scripture" (Postscript to this volume); "The Contemporaneity of the Bible," *Princeton Seminary Bulletin* 62 (1969): 38–50; and *The Living Word of the Bible* (Philadelphia: Westminster Press, 1979). The last is a series of explorations in biblical interpretation. Turn also to writings by Walter Brueggemann, one of the creative biblical theologians of our time. Note especially those books of his listed at the end of the Introduction, p. 17 above.

Method of Bible Study

Consult *Opening the Bible,* by the Trappist monk Thomas Merton (Philadelphia: Fortress Press, 1970). The creative teacher will find help from a leader in Bible study such as Hans Rudi Weber; see his *Experiments with Bible Study* (Philadelphia: Westminster Press, 1983). Consider also the special approach of Walter Wink, in *The Bible in Human Transformation: Towards a New Paradigm for Biblical Study* (Philadelphia: Fortress Press, 1973). Helpful suggestions for leading small Bible-study groups are given by Roberta Hestenes in *Using the Bible in Groups* (Philadelphia: Westminster Press, 1985).

Commentaries

In general, the commentaries in the Old Testament Library (Philadelphia: Westminster Press) and the Interpretation series (Atlanta: John Knox Press) are useful. See also the one-volume commentaries listed at the end of the Introduction above, as well as the Collegeville Bible Commentary (Old Testament, 25 volumes, Collegeville, Minn.: Liturgical Press, 1985–86), in which each volume includes the New American Bible translation of the biblical book(s), on which brief commentary and study questions are provided. The Collegeville Bible Commentary is clearly written by Roman Catholic scholars for general readers, for the self-study of the Bible, and for adult religious-education programs. The classic devotional guide is William Barclay's *The Daily Study Bible: New Testament* (revised edition, 18 volumes; Philadelphia: Westminister Press, 1975–76). See also the multiauthor Old Testament counterpart, *The Daily Study Bible: Old Testament*, for which John C. L. Gibson is general editor (24 volumes; Philadelphia: Westminster Press, 1981).

Translations

It is important to encourage participants in Bible study to consult more than one translation, and even to wonder about differences in translation. Turn to a scholar for help when necessary. The following translations are recommended:

Revised Standard Version. An ecumenical version in the tradition of the Authorized or King James Version. Highly recommended. A new, improved translation is expected in the not too distant future.

New English Bible. This translation is fresh and illuminating, though often it will offer free, idiomatic renderings.

New International Version. A beautiful translation by a team of conservative, evangelical scholars.

Jerusalem Bible. An excellent translation by Roman Catholic scholars under the sponsorship of the Ecole Biblique in Jerusalem.

Tanakh. An excellent translation under the auspices of the Jewish Publication Society of America.

New American Bible. Another fine translation by Roman Catholic scholars, with a new revised version of the New Testament.

Postscript: The Dramatic Movement of Scripture*

OUT OF MY LIFE AND THOUGHT

The topic "The Dramatic Movement of Scripture" is a loaded one! It suggests that, on the analogy of a drama, there is some sort of unity within the manifest diversity of Scripture, that a dynamic movement or development takes place within the horizons of beginning and end, and that crucial events occur at the climax or denouement which give meaning to the whole. For the Jewish community, what are decisive are the events of the exodus and at Sinai, and the unfolding tradition based on those "root experiences." For the Christian community, the crucial event, which is related in some sense to the Jewish tradition, is the Christ Event—the life, death, and resurrection of Jesus Christ—and the unfolding meaning of this turning point in history.

Since I want to speak autobiographically on this occasion, let me begin by confessing that this dramatic view of Scripture was not given to me by a direct, unprejudiced reading of the Bible itself; rather, the church has given me this *discrimen,* this way of reading the Bible. It was not, however, a teaching of the church: the way of perceiving was given to me subtly, indirectly, and indeed despite the poor preaching, teaching, and liturgy to which I was exposed.

I grew up in rural Protestantism, which gave me a naive view of Scripture which in college I had to reject—and I almost threw out the

---

*A presentation by Bernhard W. Anderson at Union Theological Seminary, New York City, in a panel discussion during the Biblical Jubilee, April 9, 1987, in celebration of the sesquicentennial of the seminary.

89

baby with the bathwater! Despite the weaknesses of evangelical Protestantism, however, I was given very early in life some sense—inadequate as it was—of the power of the gospel centering in Jesus and his role in the biblical story.

A decisive moment in my appreciation of the dramatic character of Scripture occurred in the late forties and early fifties when I was drawn into the Student Christian Movement—the SCM in the United States, and the larger World Student Christian Federation centered in Geneva. In those days, believe it or not, students gathered together in Bible study groups, and ecumenical conferences included Bible study in their programs. The assumption was that as we gather around the Bible, which in some sense is authoritative, we may wrestle with the purpose of life and be drawn together in closer unity. It was students who pressed the theologians with the larger question of the relation of the parts to the whole, of the episodes to the "unfolding drama of the Bible," in the words of the title of this book, which I wrote in the early 1950s in cooperation with students at Bucknell University.

A third influence on my understanding of Scripture comes from my growing appreciation of "the holy catholic church," to use the language of the Apostles' Creed: its majestic creeds, its rich symbolism, its engaging liturgy. There is something very dramatic about worship when it is truly worship and not an experiment, and this is related to the vision—celebrated in worship, in art, in music—of what Amos Wilder has called "the great story and plot of all time and space." With the sensitivity of a poet—and one should be a poet to understand the Bible—Wilder has observed that the biblical narratives "locate us in the very midst of the great story and plot of all time and space, and therefore relate us" to God, "the great dramatist and storyteller."[1]

STORY AND HISTORY IN
THE BIBLE

Now, this view of Scripture, given to me by the church, is not alien to Scripture itself, though it has been difficult to maintain it in the face of the critical studies of biblical scholarship.

In the past, one way of viewing the dramatic movement of Scripture has been as *Heilsgeschichte,* the history of God's redemptive purpose.

---

1. Amos Wilder, *The Language of the Gospel* (New York: Harper & Row, 1964), 64–65.

This view goes back into the New Testament itself (for example, to Luke and, in a profounder sense, Paul). It was picked up by Irenaeus in the second century and came into its own in a line of theologians extending from Johannes Cocceius in the seventeenth century to Oscar Cullmann and Gerhard von Rad in our own time.

It is no longer fashionable to speak of the dramatic movement of Scripture as *Heilsgeschichte;* and, I can agree if the history of salvation means a kind of objective history, manifest in a sequence of events, which moves inexorably through the Old Testament period to the New. For one thing, the discontinuity between the Old Testament and the New is too deep to allow for any simplistic historical understanding. For another thing, historical criticism has driven us to the realization that God's purpose cannot be traced in a sequence of historical events (a "history" in the ordinary sense) or in a reconstruction of historical events. All of this prompted one of my students to raise the question in a term paper dealing with the future of biblical theology, "Is there life after *Heilsgeschichte?*"

Nevertheless, a dramatic reading of the Bible—one that engages the imagination and appeals to the reader or hearer to be involved in the story—is rooted in Scripture itself.

In a profound sense, the Bible presents the story of a "pilgrim people"—to use an expression from the documents of the Second Vatican Council—a people who are summoned to be on the move toward God's future. This story is curiously mixed with the "history" of Israel and the "history" of the early church, showing that it is not divorced from the concrete circumstances of human life in all their tragedy and triumph, in all their sinfulness and faith. This story is not just ancient history, shut up in the dead and unrecoverable past, but a living tradition, an ongoing story in which God continues to speak anew to the people—as my Old Testament colleagues James A. Sanders and Walter Brueggemann have been saying in their respective ways. And when the Christian community rereads this story of the pilgrim people it does so not under the supposition that the story is about someone else but rather as "our story"—"the story of our life," as H. Richard Niebuhr has put it.[2]

Moreover, in a larger sense this story is not just a story about the people of God, Israel, and—correlated with it in God's elective

---

2. H. Richard Niebuhr, *The Meaning of Revelation* (New York: Macmillan Co., 1941), chap. 2.

purpose—the church. The story is part of a much larger story involving all humanity and all creation—a "cosmic journey" that moves from creation to consummation, from first things to last things.

I was surprised to read recently in a current book on Christian theology that the traditional *heilsgeschichtliche* view of the movement from creation to consummation, which has dominated the life and worship of the church ever since Irenaeus, has been called into question by historical criticism. Modern methods have allegedly demonstrated that, for instance, Genesis 1–3 is only a story, with no foundation in the actual history of the ancient world.

The conclusion follows only if one supposes that the "literal sense" of Scripture is the same as the "historical sense" as construed by historical criticism, and if the "literal sense" excludes, or rules out, a poetic sense that appeals to the imagination and becomes the shared symbolism of a community of faith. It is too bad that the "eclipse of biblical narrative," to allude to the title of Hans Frei's book,[3] has meant a loss of the vision that has fired the imagination down through the centuries: the vision of the involvement of all humanity, and indeed all creatures, in an unfolding drama extending from God's creation to the consummation of God's purpose for the creation.

CONCLUSION

I here return to the point where I began: this reading of Scripture as a dramatic movement from creation to consummation, and the story of the people of God with its denouement—according to Jewish conviction, in the exodus and at Sinai and in the unfolding of the meaning of those events, and according to Christian conviction, in the life, death, and resurrection of Jesus Christ—is celebrated primarily in worship. The Bible belongs to the community of faith!

Abraham Joshua Heschel, the distinguished Jewish philosopher who once taught at Jewish Theological Seminary, has helped me understand this. Heschel said that "the Bible is not a book to be read but a drama in which to participate."[4] Surely in its own way the Christian commu-

---

3. Hans Frei, *The Eclipse of Biblical Narrative: A Study in Eighteenth and Nineteenth Century Hermeneutics* (New Haven: Yale University Press, 1974).

4. Abraham Joshua Heschel. *God in Search of Man: A Philosophy of Judaism* (New York: Farrar, Straus & Giroux, 1976), 254.

nity shares this conviction in worship. The central rite of the Christian community, corresponding to the Passover in the Jewish community, is the Eucharist. It is a remembrance and celebration of the crucial moment of the biblical drama—and indeed in Christian vision of all history—and at the same time an invitation to participate in and bear witness to the new creation already introduced through Jesus Christ.